Beyond Beatmatching:
Take Your DJ Career to the Next Level

Written by Yakov Vorobyev and Eric Coomes
Edited by Bill Murphy

Thank you for purchasing this book.

Please visit our website to see more of our work:
www.MixedInKey.com

Authors: Yakov Vorobyev and Eric Coomes
Editor: Bill Murphy

Internet: http://mixedinkey.com/book
Email: contact@mixedinkey.com

First Edition

About the Authors

Yakov Vorobyev is the creator and founder of Mixed In Key, which has grown to become the DJ industry standard for key detection software. Vorobyev grew up in Washington, D.C., where he discovered a dual passion for writing computer code and DJing; while he worked by day at Bethesda Softworks (creators of The Elder Scrolls video game series) and various technology firms, he took to DJing by night at the top clubs in the city. In 2005, he graduated from George Washington University with a degree in Computer Science. He currently lives and works in Miami Beach, where he manages an international team of software developers to create new tools for DJs.

Eric Coomes is a forward-thinking DJ, nightlife consultant, event marketer and copywriter. After graduating magna cum laude from William Jewell College in 2003, he spent six years working at Cerner Corporation in copywriting, interactive/web design and marketing. In 2009, he turned his passion and hobby into a career, leaving Cerner to DJ full time. Eric currently holds DJ residencies at several nightclubs and DJs at philanthropic events around Kansas City. In 2011, he worked with the LAVO New York marketing team to help execute events for Sidney Samson, A-Trak, Tiësto and LMFAO.

In addition to DJing, Eric is currently a copywriter for Mixed In Key, the award-winning DJ software company.

About the Editor

Bill Murphy is a freelance writer based in New York City, and has contributed to Time Out New York, Guitar World, Bass Player, The Wire, Remix, Electronic Musician and other outlets. From 1996 to 2003, he ran producer Bill Laswell's Axiom label, distributed through Island Def Jam and Chris Blackwell's Palm Pictures.

Table of Contents

1. Introduction

Since 2006, we've helped thousands of people learn new DJ techniques. During that time, we've also communicated closely with our fans, and we've noticed that they often ask questions like: "How can I use harmonic mixing in my DJ sets?" "What is the best MacBook for DJing?" or "How do I get booked in large nightclubs?"

Our goal is to help you become an incredible DJ. We're in a unique position to help, because we create software for professional DJs. Our customers include superstars like David Guetta, who has millions of fans on Facebook, as well as up-and-coming DJs who are just starting out. We've always encouraged our community to ask questions, and we decided to give back what we've learned through experience with this easy-to-read book. We want to teach you something new, useful and exciting, regardless of your skill level.

In *Beyond Beatmatching*, we'll take an in-depth look at harmonic mixing and other techniques used by the world's top DJs. We'll explain how to make club management happy, and how you can adjust your DJ sets for different venues and crowds.

Eric and I have met and spoken with a lot of DJs over the years, and we think we have a good idea of what makes certain artists stand out. We'll talk about what makes a DJ memorable. We'll also show you how to use social media to build a larger fan base. And to help us tell our story, we've interviewed some of the top innovators in the business. Each one of them has plenty to say about how you can succeed in the art of DJing.

Finally, we'll take an in-depth look at the nightlife industry. We want to show you what happens behind the scenes in a nightclub. We'll share advice on how to get booked at clubs and festivals, as well as tips on what you need to do to land that coveted spot for all DJs: the club residency.

It's a powerful feeling when you're playing music for an audience. You're the maestro performing a masterpiece. That's why we became DJs, and that's why we love what we do. It's an incredible high, and it's even more incredible when you can predict how the crowd will react before you mix the next song. When you can tap into that shared emotion and bring everyone with you, you're not just DJing anymore; you're traveling together.

Your journey begins here, with *Beyond Beatmatching*.

2. How to Use Harmonic Mixing

Are DJs really musicians? The debate has raged for so long, you could probably sample and loop that question and make a song out of it in response. Even the Foo Fighters' Dave Grohl got into the act at the 2012 Grammy Awards, when he took a subtle swipe at DJs during his acceptance speech for Best Rock Performance. "Singing into a microphone and learning to play an instrument and learning to do your craft, that's the most important thing for people to do," he said. "It's not about being perfect, it's not about sounding absolutely correct, and it's not about what goes on in a computer."

What he forgot to mention is that for the last decade, technological advances in audio engineering have actually made it *easier* to learn your craft and pursue your dreams as a musician—even for a rocker like Dave Grohl. For this very reason, DJing has become more musically diverse as an art. When you hear BT or deadmau5 or Skrillex do a set, they're not just playing records; they're also dropping in synth lines, triggering effects, looping and manipulating beats—in short, they're *performing*, and their DJ setup is their musical instrument.

If you want to get to this level, you have to begin somewhere. We're convinced that a technique called harmonic mixing is a great place to start.

A Step Beyond Beatmatching

First, it helps to dig into a little history. To understand the roots of modern club DJing, you have to go back to New York City in the early '70s. Francis Grasso was a DJ at the famed Sanctuary nightclub, where he would spin a mixture of funk, rock and soul hits by James Brown, the Doobie Brothers, the Supremes and the Jackson 5, to name just a few. Grasso was the first DJ to use headphones so he could hear the incoming selection on one turntable and, using a fader knob, blend it into the outgoing track on the other. Up until then, most DJs were just playing one song after the next, without mixing them. "You couldn't adjust speeds," said Grasso. "You had to catch it at the right moment. There was no room for error, and you couldn't play catch up."[1]

He didn't know it then, but Grasso had invented the modern-day art of beatmatching. Today, it's one of the most basic techniques in a DJ's repertoire. Like any skill, it

---

[1] Tim Lawrence. *Love Saves the Day: A History of American Dance Music Culture, 1970-1979* (Durham, NC: Duke University Press, 2004), 36.

takes practice to get it right. So once you've crossed that bridge, how can you take that knowledge a step further and bring some real musicality into your set?

This is where harmonic mixing comes in. When you're in the middle of your set and playing one of your favorite tracks, sometimes you'll find yourself searching through your music collection, trying to figure out the right thing to play next. Harmonic mixing can help you do it. It virtually guarantees that your next track will complement the one you're playing, and that your mix will sound musically seamless.

It sounds like magic, but it's a real DJ technique with roots in music theory, and it's used by some of the world's most popular DJs, including Above & Beyond, Armin van Buuren, David Guetta, Kaskade, Markus Schulz, Sasha, Swedish House Mafia and many more. If you already know how to DJ, you can start using harmonic mixing in a matter of minutes. It's even a lot easier to learn than beatmatching.

What Is Harmonic Mixing?

Put simply, harmonic mixing helps ensure that your song transitions won't clash, and it also opens up a wealth of possibilities for creative mixes.

What it is:

- A way to improve your DJ sets

- A creative way to mix songs together

- An easy-to-learn technique that helps you sound perfect every time you play

What it's not: a law of mixing. All rules are meant to be broken. Harmonic mixing isn't a requirement to be a good DJ. It's merely a useful technique to combine with the rest of your knowledge and skills.

There are three elements to harmonic mixing:

- Analyzing your music files to figure out their musical key

- Labeling all your music with the key results, so you can find the key quickly

- Knowing which keys sound good together, and mixing with that in mind

Harmonic mixing also doesn't mean you're mixing in the same key for the entire night; instead, it means you're mixing two songs together that are harmonically compatible.

The good news is that with the software and hardware available today, it's really easy to do. As you work with the technique and train your ear to know when a mix is working musically, you'll find that it can pay huge dividends on the dance floor.

Thankfully, you don't have to study music theory to learn harmonic mixing. All you really need to know is that virtually every song you play as a DJ is in a certain key. Key names always start with the name of the root note (such as "C") and the scale (minor). The scales are usually minor or major, so you will see key names like "D flat minor" and "E major" throughout this book.

If you're not already familiar with musical keys, it will take a little time for you to learn the basics. Even if you're not trying to mix harmonically, you might get lucky if, for example, you're mixing a solo lead vocal over a monophonic (single-note) synth line. But when you're mixing chords over chords, involving *clusters* of notes, you can run into dissonance, and that's a bad thing. When mixing harmonically, you want both songs to sound as though they could have been part of the same piece of music, with a transition that feels smooth and natural. There's an art to doing it right, and when you pull it off, your audience will sense it.

Mixed In Key: Finding the Keys of Your Music

After years of watching DJs like Sasha and Paul van Dyk, Mixed In Key founder Yakov Vorobyev could tell that they were mixing harmonically. Their sets were always flawless, but it wasn't obvious how they found the various keys their tracks were in. The common method was to use a piano to find a song's key beforehand, and then label each piece of vinyl accordingly—a thankless and time-consuming grind.

As a DJ himself, Yakov was spinning several nights per week, and he used the piano method to label all his tracks. Mixed In Key software was conceived as a solution to this problem. Why do all this work by hand, when it was possible to analyze and catalogue your entire music library without ever touching a piano?

In 2006, Yakov created Mixed In Key 1.0, which analyzed music files to determine the key of each song in seconds. The software was launched as a digital download on Mixed In Key's website (mixedinkey.com). Since then, the software has been updated over 20 times; version 5.0 was released in late 2011.

Mixed In Key is a DJ tool that makes it easy to explore your music collection and find songs in the same or compatible keys. It also tags their metadata, so the results will show up on all your favorite DJ software and hardware. For its ease and elegance, and for the time it has saved professional DJs, Mixed In Key has become the industry standard for harmonic mixing.

Visual Guide: Mixing with the Camelot Wheel

Once you know the key of your music, you can start using that information to mix harmonically. The Camelot Wheel, invented by Mark Davis and part of Mixed In Key, is a color-coded system that helps you figure out which keys are compatible. Each key is assigned a code number from one to twelve, like the hours around a clock. The wheel is visually designed to help you learn harmonic mixing.

Here's what it looks like:

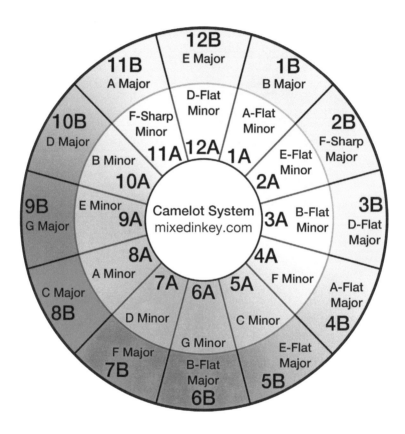

You'll notice the wheel is comprised of two concentric circles; major keys are on the outer circle and minor keys are on the inner circle.

You can start experimenting as soon as you've labeled your first ten songs with a Camelot key code. The most basic trick is to try mixing two copies of the same song. If you load up two copies of Kaskade & deadmau5's "Move For Me," for example, and then mix them, they will beatmatch perfectly, and they'll be in the same key, with the notes and harmonies in consonance.

You'll notice the same thing when you start using harmonic mixing with two different songs in the same Camelot key code (let's say 5A). Load up two songs and mix back and forth between them. That's harmonic mixing in action, with the pitch and chords in harmony.

After you've tried mixing two songs in the same key code, try a mix that's off-key. If you play a song in 5A and mix it into a song with a 10A key code, for example, you'll notice the difference immediately. The clashing pitch between the two songs creates an uncomfortable dissonance.

Finally, try mixing two songs that are in different but harmonically compatible keys. It's easy to determine a compatible key; for any key on the Camelot Wheel, the three immediately adjacent keys are compatible. So for example, let's say you've started a mix with Kaskade's "Angel On My Shoulder." This song is in the key of A minor, which is 8A on the Camelot Wheel. That means you can mix it with any other track in 7A, 8A, 9A or 8B, and feel confident that the result will be a smooth harmonic transition.

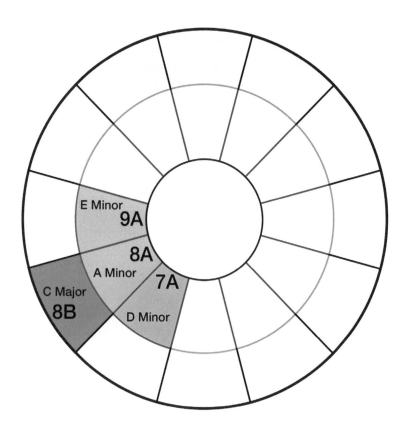

Interview with Mark Davis: Inventor of the Camelot Wheel

Mark Davis aimed to simplify the technique of harmonic mixing by making the relationships between different keys easier to remember. In January 2012, we asked him about the history of the harmonic mixing method.

Mark, what started the harmonic mixing movement in the 1980s?

MD: When I started DJing during the 1970s disco craze, I quickly learned the importance of mixing skills. Extended versions made some tracks more mixable, especially when remix services such as Hot Tracks offered versions of hit songs with extended intro and outro segments. As DJs polished their beatmixing skills, however, those with musical sense soon found that certain mixes sounded poor no matter how tightly tracks were beatmatched. This dissonance inspired DJs to consider harmonic compatibility.

In 1986, a visionary named Stuart Soroka introduced the DJ world to the concept of harmonic mixing. He published *Harmonic Keys* magazine in Key West, Florida, and rapidly expanded a subscriber base through advertising in DJ magazines such as *Dance Music Report*. The most advanced DJs of that period soon learned the value of mixing in key: It allowed them to complete the sonic tapestries they sought to create, but in which they had been thwarted by the realities of incompatible keys.[2]

Your Camelot idea changed DJing for the better. How did you get the inspiration for it?

MD: It was difficult to memorize the Harmonic Keys Overlay Chart, which listed the four perfectly compatible keys for any given key. I had an epiphany in 1991, however, which revealed that the chart could also be displayed in a circle, like the face of a clock. If I assigned numbers to each key, then I wouldn't have to memorize key relationships because finding compatible keys would be as easy as telling time. I named it the "Easymix System" and soon discovered that it was an improvement over the original 17th-century circle of fifths.

Is It Possible to Mix Harmonically Without Realizing It?

Chances are you've probably mixed harmonically before you even knew about the Camelot Wheel. There are 24 possible keys, so there's a 1 in 24 chance that if you choose any two random songs, they will be in exactly the same key. Those are low odds, but it does happen. Out of curiosity,

---

[2] Mark Davis. Camelot Sound (history section). Accessed March 12, 2012. http://www.camelotsound.com/History.aspx.

we did some original research and ran a simulation on 17,000 songs to see what the chances were of two songs being in the same key if chosen at random. The results confirmed what we had anticipated: for every 1 in 24 choices, or 4.16 percent of the time, the two songs were in the same key.

Instead of just taking a chance on your mix being harmonic, the Camelot system ensures that you'll get a smooth transition every time.

Summary of Harmonic Mixing

To sum up, here's how you can use the Camelot Wheel to guarantee that your mixes are harmonically correct:

1. Determine the Camelot key of each track (e.g., 5A).

2. Label your entire collection so you can see the Camelot key code for all the songs you play. (Mixed In Key does steps 1 and 2 for you.)

3. Every time you mix between songs in the same key, it'll sound perfect. For example, when you mix a track in 5A into another track in 5A, this mix will always be in key.

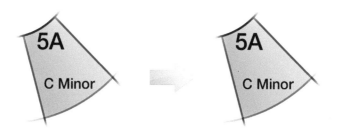

4. For compatible mixes, think of the numbers on the Camelot Wheel like the hours on a clock. Go forward or backward one hour, and you'll have a harmonically compatible mix. So if you're in 5A, you can mix into 4A or 6A.

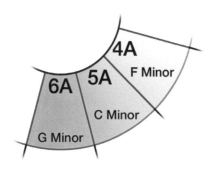

5. You can also change the letter but keep the same number, and your mix will still be compatible. For example, 5A can mix into 5B, and 5B can mix back into 5A.

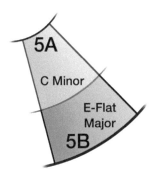

6. Any time you're mixing, you have four possible compatible keys to choose from. You can stay in the same key, you can add or subtract one "hour," or you can switch from A to B and from B to A.

We encourage you to try different Camelot combinations so you can become familiar with how the Camelot Wheel works. We've heard from many of the DJs we work with that this concept has changed the industry, because it makes their mixes sound incredibly musical. We think you'll come to the same conclusion.

Extra tip: Since the Camelot Wheel is color-coded, we find it useful to remember that if the latest Axwell track is in the key of 10A, for example, its color code will be blue. When you remember the color code, it's easier to remember which tracks will mix well together.

3. Integrate Mixed In Key with Your DJ Gear

As a DJ, you can use music to form a deep connection with your audience. You can tell a story, create an atmosphere, and take your listeners on a journey with you. The beauty of a well-crafted mix is that the sum is greater than the individual parts. Two DJs can play the same song, but it will sound totally different—and elicit a different reaction— in the context of a mix.

It's also useful to keep in mind that certain keys can evoke specific feelings. For example, C minor can sound romantic and whimsical, while D major can sound triumphant, and D minor can sound gloomy.[3] Generally speaking, major scales sound happy and elated (think of a peak-time David Guetta anthem), while minor scales sound sad and wistful (think of Adele's "Someone Like You").[4]

---

[3] Christian Schubart. "Affective Key Characteristics." Accessed January 30, 2012. http://www.wmich.edu/mus-theo/courses/keys.html.

[4] Michaeleen Doucleff. "Anatomy of a Tear Jerker," *Wall Street Journal.* Accessed February 11, 2012. http://online.wsj.com/article/SB10001424052970203646004577213010291701378.html.

David Guetta, *DJ Mag*'s 2011 Top 100 poll winner, has achieved success because his music contains harmonies that trigger a real emotional connection with his listeners.[5] But what happens when you choose an uplifting, upbeat Guetta track in the key of C major and mix it with a darker track in the key of D minor? You might lose your audience completely and end up clearing the dance floor.

We created Mixed In Key so you can keep up that energy and still keep moving forward creatively. We think it's vital for DJs to be able to experiment with harmonic relationships in their mixes. DJing is very much a musical art form, and harmonic mixing adds an exciting dimension to it.

---

[5] *Last Call with Carson Daly*, NBC. Accessed January 30, 2012. http://www.nbc.com/last-call-with-carson-daly/video/david-guetta/1358467.

Harmonic Mixing with Your DJ Setup

Now that you understand what harmonic mixing is, you're just a few simple steps away from being able to use it with your DJ software. The easiest way to get started is to run your music through Mixed In Key, and then update your DJ software to show the key of each song you import. The key is notated in our Camelot format. This is the typical process for most DJs:

Once your songs are labeled, it's a good idea to organize them by key, or to create separate playlists with tracks that are harmonically compatible. As we noted in Chapter 2, the Camelot Wheel is designed to give you a deeper understanding of song keys and how they relate to each other. For a playable version, go to http://camelotwheel.com, where you'll find brief demos of harmonic mixes. You can also experiment with mixes on your own by clicking on different parts of the wheel.

We can't emphasize enough how important it is to familiarize yourself with these harmonic relationships. Club environments can be hectic, so it's to your advantage to be prepared in case you have to select tracks on the fly. Take a lesson from Kaskade, who labels all his music in advance. When he's in a club or playing a festival gig in front of thousands of screaming fans, he doesn't have to worry about conflicting keys in his mixes because he's done all the preparation beforehand.

Labeling Your iTunes Library

If you use iTunes to organize your music library—and we know many DJs who do—then you can use Mixed In Key to label your tracks so their key information shows up in iTunes. This is a pretty simple process:

1. In Mixed In Key, go to **Personalize**, click on **Update Tags**, select **Store Key Result** and choose **Before Comments**. Add your MP3 and MP4 files and process them.

2. Open iTunes and select the files you have analyzed. Right click on the selection and choose **Get Info**. Type a single character in one of the empty tag fields that you don't plan on using, check the checkbox next to it, and click **OK**. This forces iTunes to refresh itself.

3. After iTunes refreshes your library, your Mixed In Key results will appear in the **Comments** column.

Updating Your DJ Software

We've worked with all the major DJ software, and have outlined below the steps you need to take to use each one with Mixed In Key. No matter which software you use, once your music is tagged properly, harmonic mixing is a snap.

Native Instruments' Traktor

1. For MP3 and MP4 (iTunes) files, we recommend going to **Personalize** in Mixed In Key, click on **Update Tags** and enabling **Update Initial Key Tag**. For all other file types, we recommend storing the key **Before Comments**.

2. Add your files to Mixed In Key and process them.

3. Open Traktor and select the files you have analyzed. Right click on the selection and choose **Check Consistency** from the pop-up menu. Your keys should now appear in Traktor.

Serato Scratch Live and ITCH

1. For MP3 files, we recommend going to **Personalize**, then **Update Tags** in Mixed In Key and enabling **Update Initial Key Tag**. For all other file types, we recommend storing the key **Before Comments**.

2. Add your files to Mixed In Key and process them.

3. Open Serato and press the **Files** button. Inside Serato's browser, drag the files you analyzed with Mixed In Key onto the **Rescan ID3 Tags** button. Your keys should now appear in Serato.

Pioneer CDJs with Rekordbox

1. For MP3 files, we recommend going to **Personalize**, then **Update Tags** in Mixed In Key and enabling **Update Initial Key Tag**. For all other file types, we recommend storing the key **Before Comments**.

2. Add your files to Mixed In Key and process them.

3. Open rekordbox and select the files you have analyzed. Right click on the selection, and choose **Reload Tags** from the pop-up menu. Your keys should now appear in rekordbox.

Ableton Live

Ableton Live is a little harder to use for harmonic mixing than other DJ software because it doesn't show the metadata for each file. Here are three successful approaches that we've discovered:

1. Use Mixed In Key as a browser and drag-and-drop clips from Mixed In Key into Ableton Live.

2. For each key that's on your hard drive, create separate folders in Live (for example, 1A, 1B, 2A, 2B, and so on). Then drag and drop files from Mixed In Key into their corresponding folders in Live.

3. For Live experts only: enable **File Renaming** in Mixed In Key to add the key to the file name. The keys will show up in Live in the title of each clip. You will not lose warp markers since the software renames the associated .ASD files, but any Live projects that contain the original files will stop working. That's the last thing you want to happen when you show up at a club.

Extra tip: Once again, preparation is essential in harmonic mixing, so make it easy on yourself. Whatever DJ hardware or software you use, make sure you can see your key labels clearly, even in a dark club environment.

4. Visualize the Structure of Dance Music

Remember Francis Grasso, the godfather of beatmatching who introduced a sense of musicality to the art of DJing? Well, to save time and streamline his mixing process, Grasso came up with another technique that became a secret weapon for many top DJs in the analog age. To put it simply, Grasso taught himself how to *read* records.

"If you look at a [vinyl] album carefully," he explained, "you can see which parts of it are vocal and which parts are musical, so you've already got a head start. The dark black grooves are instrumental sections and the lighter black is the vocal."[6]

Nowadays, whether you prefer CDs, vinyl, digital DJ setups or even MP3 DJ gadgets, the only thing that matters is how you use what you've got. The gear and the medium may be different, but the demands of today's audiences are the same: They want to be thrilled by what they're hearing. In this chapter, we'll explain how you can create more

---

[6] Tim Lawrence. *Love Saves the Day: A History of American Dance Music Culture, 1970-1979* (Durham, NC: Duke University Press, 2004), 36.

exciting buildups and transitions in your set by visualizing the structure of the songs you're mixing.

The Structure of a Typical Track

Most popular dance music follows a basic structure that's easy to learn. If you understand a song's structure—the way its sections have been arranged to create the total work—then you're getting closer to understanding how a song can *connect*, emotionally, with its listener. That's powerful information for a DJ to have.

Ideally, a well-crafted song structure will create an immediate experience for you as a listener, telling a story with a sense of anticipation that builds toward an emotional release, burning the song into your memory. The song's different parts—verse, chorus and bridge—are all arranged and repeated to help tell this story and make the song more memorable. Once you can visualize a song's structure, as a DJ you have the elements at your fingertips to create a seamless transition between songs without losing a crowd's energy.

Here is how a typical song is structured:

Intro: An intro is typically a multiple of 16 beats in length, and often introduces a new instrument or sound every 32 beats. Some intros open with drums and gradually add layers of instruments. A buildup or other aural cue lets you know it's over.

Verse: In songs with lyrics, each verse is usually different from the next. The verse sets up the theme of the song and builds a natural progression to the chorus.

Chorus: This contains the main message or theme of the song. It's built around a melodic "hook" and is the most catchy and energetic part of the song.

Breakdown: This is a transition from the end of the chorus to the beginning of the next part of the song. Dance tracks tend not to include percussion during the breakdown.

Verse 2: Most songs contain a second verse with different lyrics.

Chorus 2: Usually, the second chorus repeats the first chorus.

Bridge: This is an optional transitional section near the end of a song, most often in pop music. A bridge will occur only once, and musically and lyrically it's different from the rest of the song.

Chorus 3: Some tracks will repeat the chorus a third time.

Outro: This is the closing segment, where the song fades or breaks down to simple beats. It's most likely the same length as the intro.[7]

If you understand these structural elements and how they relate to each other, you'll know exactly where you are at any point in a particular track. As a DJ, knowing when the tune is playing a verse, a chorus, or a breakdown—even if the song has no lyrics—can help you create seamless, professional mixes. In turn, this knowledge will help you get creative with your mix. (For example, at the right moment, you can drop in the chorus of a harmonically compatible song, which is one of the basic elements of a mashup. We'll get into more of this in Chapter 7.)

Beats

Most dance music tracks open with what's often called a "four-on-the-floor" rhythm, with the kick drum bumping out a steady *boom boom boom boom*. Each *boom* is a beat. It sounds obvious, but when you nod your head or tap your foot, you're really just keeping time with the beat.

---

[7] Ibid., 229.

You're probably very familiar with this concept already, but it's worth mentioning because it sneaks up in different ways. When you look at a DJ mixer, for example, and see a value like "1/16" on an effects knob, it means the effect is designed to modulate or repeat every 1/16th of a beat. A value of "4" indicates four beats, or more simply, a *bar*. Slow flange effects will often modulate every 16 or 32 beats.

Phrases

A phrase is a segment of music, whether a melody or a rhythm, that has a complete musical sense of its own. Put more simply, it has a natural sense of *structural completeness*— a beginning, a middle and an end. For example, you might hear a synth melody that repeats multiple times. Each repetition is probably a phrase; it usually consists of 32 or 64 beats (8 or 16 bars), but it can be shorter. It's like a sentence, where each beat is like a word.

Each phrase begins with a unique element, like a cymbal crash or the start of a melody. From a listener's standpoint, this is a cue that the songwriter or producer has left for you to discover, so you know where you are in the track.

Once you get used to thinking about beats and phrases, and their place in song structure, you'll notice that almost all the popular music in the world follows the formula we've described above. It just feels comfortable and natural. And once you can identify end-of-phrase markers instinctively, you won't need to count out beats and phrases; instead, you'll *feel it* when the music is about to change.

What is Active Listening?

It's one thing to hear music; it's another thing entirely to *listen* to it. This means focusing your attention so you can begin to absorb a song's melody and structure. "Our brain relies on triggers," writes club DJ John Steventon, "such as the end-of-phrase markers, vocals or even just looking at the different heights of the waveform to help you remember the structure [of a song]."[8]

What he means is that a song contains multiple cues that help you determine where you are. Once you familiarize yourself with these cues, you'll start to access them subconsciously. The key is to listen to the song's structure with an active ear, and to pin down such elements as the melody, the hook, and the start of a new phrase. By training yourself to pay attention to each element and what comes next, eventually you'll be able to navigate your way through the different sections of a song instinctively.

---

[8] John Steventon. DJing for Dummies (West Sussex, England: John Wiley & Sons, Ltd., 2010), 231.

Waveforms

As Francis Grasso discovered back in the early days of vinyl, you can actually see a song's waveform on the record itself. The darker parts of the vinyl mean there's not as much information cut into the groove, so it's likely not to contain a beat.[9] Heavy bass requires cutting deeper grooves in the vinyl, and that's usually where the beats are.

Today's digital waveforms are much easier to read; in fact, it's a pretty intuitive process. As you might expect, the narrow portions denote a quiet section of the song, while

---

[9] Ibid., 204.

the tall portions are louder and typically contain drums. These distinctions add a level of detail that helps you see when a beat is about to kick in, even if it's not audible yet.

How can you use this knowledge to your advantage? Think about the effect of the contrast between the quiet and loud sections of a song like Daft Punk's "One More Time." The abrupt change from a gentle melody to a pumping beat creates an emotion that translates into energy. And that's what makes a crowd want to jump up and down.

Let's take a look at the song's waveform:

Track name: "One More Time"
Artist: Daft Punk
Tempo: 123 BPM
Key: B minor/E minor/G major
Time: 5:20

CDJs and most DJ software programs have a way to visualize an audio wave just like the image above. Notice the skinny blue area at the beginning of the waveform. The track starts out with a 64-beat intro in the key of B minor.

After the first two phrases (about 30 seconds in), you hear
the familiar "one more time" vocal, and a drumbeat begins.
32 beats later, another drum is added; after another 32
beats, vocals are added. The pink waveform indicates the
breakdown, as well as a key change to E minor and then to
G major. The track finishes with two 32-beat repeats of the
chorus.

Let's compare "One More Time" to "I Gotta Feeling"
by the Black Eyed Peas:

Track name: "I Gotta Feeling"
Artist: Black Eyed Peas
Tempo: 128 BPM
Key: C major/G major
Time: 4:49

Produced by David Guetta, the song begins with a
synthesized guitar intro. Eight bars in, will.i.am sings the
vocal "I gotta feeling," which signals the beginning of the
next phrase. A hi-hat comes in and continues for two
phrases (64 beats), but the heavy drumbeat doesn't begin
until 1:00 into the track. Note the abrupt change in the

waveform. By visualizing the music like this, you can anticipate when changes in a song are going to happen.

Now let's compare these tracks to "Smooth Criminal" by Michael Jackson:

4A

00:00 / 04:17   Smooth Criminal

Track name: "Smooth Criminal"
Artist: Michael Jackson
Tempo: 118 BPM
Key: F minor
Time: 4:17

Although this song was produced in 1988, the basic structural elements are similar to tracks being produced today. After a brief intro, you hear Michael Jackson's patented *Oooh!* followed by eight bars of the basic rhythm and melody. After another eight bars (32 beats), Michael's vocals begin.

Music production hasn't changed much since the 1980s. Even though these songs come from radically different genres and time periods, they have similar sonic qualities. That's what makes it possible to mix them.

Comparing Waveforms: DJ Sets

By looking at the audio wave of a DJ set, you can tell a lot about how it sounds. Let's examine Kaskade's "BBC Radio 1 Essential Mix," which he recorded for the BBC in London. Hosted by Pete Tong, the Essential Mix is a legendary weekly radio show on BBC Radio One. Since its start in the early 1990s, the show has championed dance music worldwide, and has featured big names like Erick Morillo, Richie Hawtin, Boys Noize, Paul van Dyk, Avicii, deadmau5, Laidback Luke, Daft Punk, Tiësto, Eric Prydz, Armin Van Buuren, Mark Knight, David Guetta, Martin Solveig, Above & Beyond and many more.

Kaskade's mix was nominated by the BBC as one of the best in 2011. Here's a waveform showing the peaks and valleys in his mix:

Notice that the audio is not consistently loud; there are constant breaks. If Kaskade played high-energy beats for two hours straight, the waveform would be a solid block.

Compare Kaskade's set to the waveform of a relatively chill opening set:

There's much more space between peaks. You can tell just by looking at the waveform of the set that it was more relaxed than Kaskade's Essential Mix.

Let's look at one more example. The Swedish House Mafia made history in December 2011 by becoming the first DJs to headline Madison Square Garden in New York City. Here's the waveform of their live set:

Does this look like it was a high-energy DJ set or a chillout mix? Without knowing anything about the artist, you can see that the mix has few valleys, leaving no doubt that this was a banging set. And what else would you expect at Madison Square Garden?

Comparing Waveforms: House and Hip-Hop

If we go back to Daft Punk's "One More Time" and use Mixed In Key to analyze it, here's what we get:

We can see that the tempo is 123 BPM, and according to the Camelot Wheel, the primary key is 10A (B minor), and the key changes to 9A/9B (E minor/G major) during the breakdown. The dynamic spacing (the relationship between loud and quiet sections) of this track differs radically from the live set waveforms we just analyzed.

Let's compare it to "Empire State of Mind" by Jay-Z and Alicia Keys:

This is in the Camelot key of 2A/2B, and the tempo is 86 BPM—much slower than the dance/house beat of "One More Time." But the differences really emerge in the waveform; because the breakdown is less essential in hip-hop, there's often little change in dynamics, so the track is mostly peaks.

These are just some of the issues you need to take into account when preparing your DJ set. Thinking about music visually—and training your ear to recognize a verse, a chorus, a breakdown or a bridge—will help you to improve the richness and complexity of your mixes. When you can get to a point where you're mixing harmonically *and* controlling the dynamics of your set, then you're bringing real *energy* to your audience.

5. Control the Energy Level

In any DJ set, ebb and flow is crucial. When you move from the ambient minimalist soundscapes of techno artists like Richie Hawtin to the banging walls of sound generated by Daft Punk or the Chemical Brothers, it's important to be aware of the change in mood and atmosphere you're demanding of your listeners. Transporting a crowd to dizzy heights and then bringing everyone down for a breather is an essential skill, and it's all about *energy control.*

Rhythm

Tempo (Italian for "time") tells us how fast a piece of music is being played or should be played. It's usually measured in beats per minute (BPM) and has a strong effect on how the mood of a particular piece of music comes across. The faster the tempo, presumably, the more emotion and urgency you're directing at the dance floor.

But *rhythm* is about more than just beats and tempo. Ideally, you want people to groove to your music for as long as possible, but you don't want to wear them out. Along those lines, we like to think of rhythm as a landscape with peaks and valleys. At the peaks, you're telling your audience when to get excited; at the valleys, you're giving them a chance to breathe. The best DJs use rhythm in this way to their advantage. Whether they're dropping in a banging percussive break during a peak, or scaling back to a lone four-on-the-floor kick during a valley, they're always thinking about managing the energy level and rhythmic flow of their set.

In Search of the Perfect Flow

Good timing is the magic that keeps people dancing. It's great to know how to beatmatch without the aid of computer software, but phrase-matching is actually a more important DJ skill. As we mentioned in Chapter 4, understanding phrasing helps you know when to start mixing out of the track you're playing and into a new one, so your mix sounds seamless.

Dance music is generally produced in groups or *phrases* of 32 beats. You'll typically hear a new musical element at the beginning of each phrase. Again, it's important to listen carefully and *actively* to identify the elements of each song you're mixing. You should almost always start a new song at the beginning of a phrase in the outgoing track. Train your ears to recognize a new phrase, and you'll know when to start the mix.

Hip-hop and pop songs often use shorter phrasing, with only an 8-beat or 16-beat intro section. You can either wait until there are only 8 or 16 beats left in the phrase of the outgoing track to begin your mix, or you can loop the intro of the track you are bringing in, to give yourself more time to extend the mix.

In general, it's a good idea to mix out of the chorus so the crowd hears the most familiar part of the song, and then continue your momentum into the next track. The first verse of your new song should start as the chorus of the outgoing track is ending or fading, so that your mixes feel natural and blend seamlessly together. If you don't pay attention to the overall phrasing, you run the risk of your mix sounding awkward and forced.

Keep in mind that the song's producers likely had a good idea of when to introduce the breakdown, so try to think about the space between, and don't eliminate any relaxation elements in the song. It's smart to avoid overlaying a beat on the breakdown; if you keep this section melodic (and free of sonic textures like white noise, synth washes, bleeps and so on), this gives people room to breathe. Even if you're playing minimal house music, try to play breakdowns with some melody.

The most basic use of phrasing is to mix the intro of one track over the outro of another track. Let's give it a try with a sample mix using the following tracks:

Nadia Ali, Starkillers, and Alex Kenji, "Pressure"
(Alesso Remix)
Camelot key: 5A

Kaskade featuring Rebecca and Fiona, "Turn It Down"
(Deniz Koyu Remix)
Camelot key: 4B

If you let "Pressure" play all the way through until the 64-beat outro, and then begin to mix in the 64-beat intro of "Turn It Down," this is what the waveforms look like:

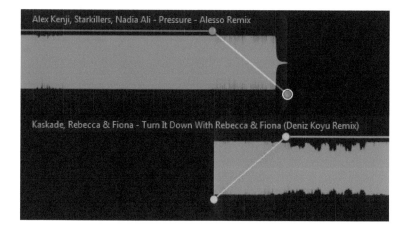

Mixing intros over outros is the simplest mix you can do. On the plus side, it's fairly easy and straightforward. The down side is that you're playing the full six minutes of each track, so your crowd might start to get bored.

One solution to the down side is to use *phrasing* to mix the beats together at an earlier portion of the song. Notice below that we didn't mix over the melodic breakdown of "Pressure," but let the chorus play through twice before beginning the mix.

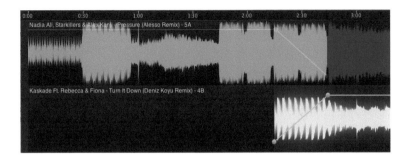

All we did here was to shorten the length of our first track. Since dance music is almost always written in 32-beat phrases, you can feel confident that the melody of "Turn It Down" will be timed to begin immediately after you have fully mixed out of "Pressure."

Mixing Is Elemental: Melody, Rhythm and Intensity

Besides beatmatching songs by tempo, you can match specific elements in a song, provided they're in the same key. Many club tracks have similar vocal elements that you can mix and match. If two songs have a similar lead vocal or even similar lyrics, you can insert one vocal where the other leaves off.

If your track is an instrumental, you can also match drumming styles. Try mixing from a song with tribal elements or conga drums over another song with similar drums. This can create a real surge of excitement, because the mix is driven entirely by the rhythm.

Varying levels of *intensity* are also essential elements in dance music. When you think of your favorite dance tracks, you'll find that most of them are structured according to this linear pattern: **intro > normal intensity > high intensity > breakdown > high intensity > outro**.

The main thing, as always, is to consider the flow of the elements you're mixing. Here are some quick tips on how to manage the intensity of a mix:

- Don't let the music play nonstop without a break. Let the **breakdown** play through and don't mix anything new over it; your audience needs a chance to rest.

- Don't mix from a **high intensity** section to an **intro**. You can lose momentum with your audience and bring them down too quickly.

- Don't mix from **breakdown** 1 into **breakdown** 2. This might work for a chillout room, but not the dance floor.

- Don't mix from a **breakdown** into the **high intensity** section of another song. It might sound too abrupt because it doesn't give your listeners enough transition time.

The best approach is to let a breakdown play all the way through. When the high intensity portion of the song comes back, you can mix into the normal or high intensity portion of the next song. This will keep your energy going.

Syncing Your Beats in Perfect Phase

Sometimes you'll hear a DJ beatmatch two songs perfectly, but the drums hit at slightly different times so there's a small gap between them. Instead of a solid *boom*, the drums start to flam, creating a *ba-boom* sound. To a professional DJ, even a few milliseconds of this mismatch can sound obvious. The key to solving the problem is to *phase* your beats correctly.

To understand what phasing is, think about two ocean waves colliding with each other. Without getting too mathematical or scientific, the waves can either add up or cancel each other out as they pass through one another. This phenomenon is called superposition[10] and phase cancellation.

---

[10] "Oceans in Motion: Waves and Tides," accessed January 30, 2012. http://kingfish.coastal.edu/biology/sgilman/770Oceansinmotion.htm.

To give you a visual example, the TV show *The Deadliest Catch* featured one of the only rogue waves (also called monster or abnormal waves) captured on video. A rogue wave occurs when the wave amplification between two smaller waves creates a wave that's much higher than what you would normally see on the ocean. In Season 2, episode you would normally see on the ocean. In Season 2, Episode 4, one of the ships in the fleet took a rogue wave that caused the ship to list on its side.[11]

This same rogue wave phenomenon applies to audio waves. When two waves peak at the same time, they're considered to be "in phase." When the peaks occur at different times, they're incoherent or "out of phase." We can illustrate this with a few examples.

---

[11] "Deadliest Catch: Tragedy at Sea," Discovery Channel, accessed January 30, 2012. http://dsc.discovery.com/videos/deadliest-catch-tragedy-at-sea.html.

Songs at different tempos:

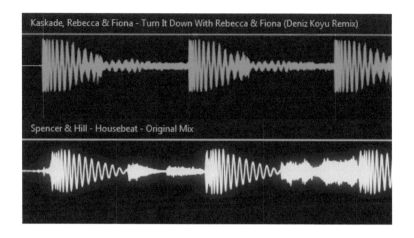

Songs at the same tempo, beatmatched and in phase (layered very close together, on the beat):

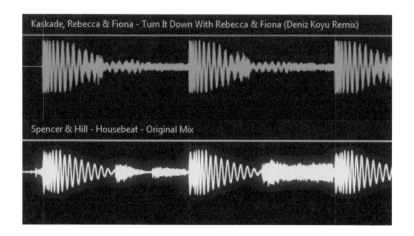

Songs at the same tempo, but out of phase:

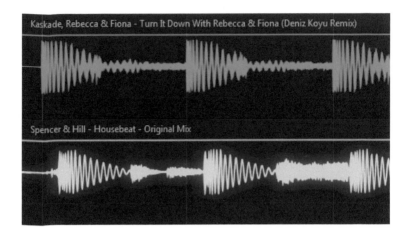

If you set up two copies of the same song and press play on both decks at the same time, chances are the two records won't be exactly in phase. When the beat is off—if the phase is too wide—it will sound like the beats are galloping separately. As a visual reference, picture Olympic sprinters on a track and what their legs look like when they're running at the same pace in perfect sync. Once they begin sprinting toward the finish line, when they're no longer in sync, they're "out of phase" with each other.

When the beats are very close to each other—if the phase is narrow but not quite perfect—you'll hear weird effects like flanging or beat cancellation. Flanging sounds like a jet taking off, which is good if you *want* that audio effect, but not good if it happens unexpectedly. Even worse, with beat cancellation, your drums will suddenly disappear. You might also get a random beat amplification effect where the beat becomes twice as loud as any other part of the song. In other words, phasing can cause havoc.

Here are some visual examples. The red and blue waves display two similar waves that are out of phase. In the context of a DJ mix, this would cause confusion on the dance floor. Your audience needs to know which beat they are dancing to; bad phasing makes them stumble and lose the groove.

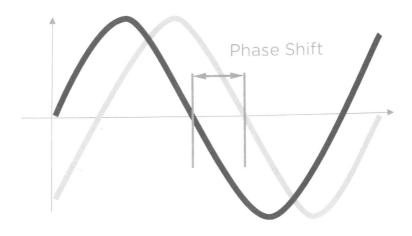

You can correct the problem in programs like Traktor or Serato by nudging the deck platter of the songs up and down, or by using the platter on the CD deck. You know `·-ᵒ succeeded when it's impossible to tell the beats

Few people realize this, but the EQ knob for "bass/low" on your mixer was invented to help correct phase problems during mixing. You can't mix two tracks together without using EQ because you usually run into wave amplification, which makes the bass too boomy. By removing the bass from one track, it makes the transition smoother.

Energy Level Mixing

We've never seen this technique described online, and since it's new to so many people, we're happy to share it with you here.

Hi-hats are often used in music to build intensity. You can think of the entire high end of the spectrum as the area with the most energy to make people dance. To test this in action, play any song you want, and cut the high frequencies with the EQ knob on your mixer. In almost every situation, the energy seems to get sucked out of the room.

The more hi-hats in a song, the more danceable it tends to become. Other sonic elements like big riffs, white noise (the elongated *shhhh* sound, akin to static) and other percussive sounds typically contribute to this energy. Conga slaps, for example, are almost exclusively in the high-frequency spectrum, which is what makes them stand out so infectiously.

The real question is how to use this information. It's pretty subjective, but for the sake of making our point, let's imagine that all the music in the world can be plotted on a "dance energy" scale of 1 to 10. If you listen to classical music, the energy level is around 1 or 2. Lounge music is 2 or 3. House music starts around 4, while Afrojack-style tracks can get as high as 9 or 10. If the song makes people jump up and down like Daft Punk's "One More Time," it's typically a 10.

Think about the music you play in your own DJ sets. Where does it fall? For our personal collection, the answer is somewhere between 5 and 8. When we play an opening set, we'll start with lower energy music in the range of level 4 to 5. During peak time, we'd play at level 8 or 9.

Again, this isn't an exact science, so you can create your own scale. Maybe you play minimal German techno—level 4 to most people, but let's say to you, it's level 9. You can choose your own numbers, but try to keep it fair. As a DJ, it helps to be brutally honest when you analyze how any track you play compares to the rest of your music collection, because you're not just playing music for yourself.

Here's an example of a Level 3 song:

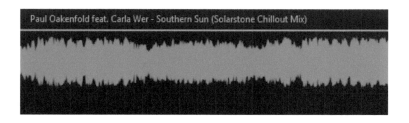

Paul Oakenfold feat. Carla Wer - Southern Sun (Solarstone Chillout Mix)

And here's an example of a Level 9 song:

Afrojack - Polkadots 2010 - Oliver Twitz Remix

When you mix with energy level in mind, it's wise to change intensity just one step at a time. As a general rule, mixing from a lower level to a higher level will liven up your dance floor, but it's a good idea to hold the throttle back a little, rather than crank it up all in one shot. If you're mixing a level 4 song, you can go into level 5, but level 9 might be too much of a jolt for your audience.

In many ways, energy level mixing is a lot like harmonic mixing. Just as the Camelot Wheel assigns a key value to tracks that are harmonically compatible, your energy level values can also inform your choices for your DJ set. And when you combine energy level mixing with harmonic mixing, you're elevating your own DJing skills into new territory.

So let's say you're playing a level 6 track in the key of 5A. You can mix into a level 7 track in 5A to get a lift in energy that also sounds *musical*. When you have that kind of control over your set, your dance floor will groove harder.

By the way, with practice, this technique will help you when you transition between different genres. If you're playing house music at 126 BPM and transition into hip-hop at 99 BPM, the energy of the floor will drop if you're not careful. So when you're about to play a slow track, make sure it has a higher energy level, and you can make the transition smoothly without losing your dance floor.

Echo and Delay

We've talked about how hi-hats and white noise can add energy to your music. You can also use your mixer's **echo** and **delay** effects to increase the current energy level of whatever you're playing.

Imagine that your current song is at level 5. If you want the crowd to get a bit more hyped-up during the second part of the track, then set your mixer's effect setting to echo, and choose a beat-synchronized value like 1/2. This effect will double the intensity of the hi-hat. You can use the beat-sync knob to fade the value up and down—so for example, if you choose 1/4, it will be four times more intense. Every time you use this effect, the perceived energy level of your song can increase by 1 or 2 points.

In general, you'll get good results when you use echo or delay, but don't go over the top. We've found that if you stick to using effects only once for every 15 songs you play, and keep the effect strength at no more than 25 percent, the change gets noticed for its uniqueness and taste, without just sounding like a gimmick. We recommend watching the dance floor when you do it too—this way you have visual cues from your audience to tell you when to stop. And lastly: this is strictly a "live performance" tip. It only comes across on a big sound system, so we don't recommend doing it for your podcasts or radio shows.

When to Chill Out

Some of the best works of art are appreciated as much for their contrast as their content. In music, professional musicians often refer to the importance of knowing when *not* to play, and the same holds true for DJing. Using breakdowns, we as DJs can create contrast in our performances, giving our audience a chance to chill out and appreciate a carefully crafted mix.

Well-placed breakdowns can be the difference between an average night and a great night. The key is to stay attuned to the dance floor. If dancers look tired, this could be your cue to highlight the contrast between a driving beat and a breakdown. An elongated breakdown gives everyone some down time, but it also creates anticipation for what's coming. When the beat finally kicks in again, the change shifts the focus back to you, ensuring that you have your audience's full attention.

There's a subtle art to pulling this off effectively. Most popular dance music is dense with sound and very light on space, so it's smart to be open to reaching across to other genres—ambient techno or even old-school drum 'n bass and dubstep, for instance—as an option for grabbing and dropping atmospheric breakdowns. Of course, with artists like Swedish House Mafia, you'll find some songs that provide ready-made space.

When you combine this approach with harmonic mixing, you'll do even better. A long melodic breakdown in a minor key will sound dark, but a long breakdown with a happy melody in a major key can really lift the crowd when the beat comes back in—especially if you step up the energy level on top of it. Always be ready to experiment, and you might surprise yourself.

Timbaland is a prime example of a producer who fully understands the concept of space. In Nelly Furtado's "Say It Right," Justin Timberlake's "Cry Me a River," and the Pussycat Dolls' "Wait a Minute," all of which he co-produced, his bass lines are not pounding every beat, but they still manage to control the song. He uses an artful and economic layering of sounds to create syncopated melodies that grab the listener with catchy hooks and well-timed breaks. He doesn't need to fill in every single beat; by leaving something out, he lets our brains fill in the gaps.

Listen to a clip of Timbaland's beat from "Say It Right" and compare it to a house beat by Swedish House Mafia. The house beat is in 4/4 time with a relentless drive, but Timbaland's beat is airy and loose, with a syncopated feeling that you rarely get in most house or electronic music.

Silence can be powerful, even if it's only for a fraction of a second. If the entire club goes quiet because you're in the middle of a beautiful breakdown, it's okay. It means that you're in control of your set, but you're also making it clear that your first concern is for your audience, and that's a good thing.

Classic Examples

Before we move on, here's a short list of some great DJ performances that illustrate how you can maintain a solid level of energy throughout your set:

- **Sasha**, Global Underground 13

- **Sasha and John Digweed**, Northern Exposure trilogy

- **Tamas Horvath**'s 15-minute entry in Mixed In Key's 2009 DJ Contest

- **Paul Oakenfold**, Tranceport

6. Find and Play Unique Tracks

More than ever, DJs are putting their personal stamp on popular dance music. Labels like Global Underground and Fabric continue to release a steady stream of remix albums and live DJ sets, while top DJs (among them BT, Sasha, David Guetta, Carl Craig, Richie Hawtin, Kaskade and many more) have made the transition to record producer, establishing an individual *sound* all their own that's in demand across the music industry.

What accounts for the wave of DJ popularity? A lot of it starts, as it always has, on the dance floor. If you can *connect* with your audience through the music you select and the way you mix it, you're on your way. Dance music covers such a wide range of genres that the possibilities are pretty much endless when it comes to approaching a DJ set; what matters is what your set says about *you* as a DJ. That means not only seeking out and finding the tracks that sound great, but also thinking in terms of how you can give your listeners the energy level they're looking for, and still assert your personality as a DJ. It's a fine balance, but this is where you can start to develop and personalize your own sound.

Crate Digging: Finding Great Music

Even after the iPod hit the market, building a music collection still meant prowling record shops and searching through stacks of CDs or vinyl. Before MP3s and social media opened up new avenues to buy and share individual songs online, DJs were willing to buy entire albums just to get the perfect song (or the perfect "break," if hip-hop was your specialty).

It's easier to access music today, but as a DJ, it's important not to sacrifice quality for convenience. If you play digital music, only the highest-quality music files will do. Low-resolution MP3s or tracks ripped from YouTube videos will sound flattened and less defined when playing through a club sound system.

WAV files store raw audio data and provide CD-quality sound at a size of about 10MB per minute of music. MP3s reduce the size of audio files by compressing and encoding data at different bitrates, measured in kilobits per second (kbps).

All music files purchased through websites like Beatport.com are downloadable as WAV or MP3 files in high-resolution 320 kbps format. You should never be satisfied with 192 kbps files if you can get a higher bitrate. In 192 kbps files, frequencies around 17 kilohertz and higher are cut off, so hi-hats sound dull compared to 320 kbps files. You won't notice the difference on your laptop speakers, but it will be obvious in a club.

Music services such as DJCity.com offer downloads in full 320 kbps quality. For a fee of $30/month, you can access unlimited downloads of all the latest dance tracks. Depending on your personal taste, you can find similar services to fit your needs. Websites like Traxsource, for example, are dedicated primarily to house music. We tend to make the majority of our purchases on Beatport, Traxsource, Amazon MP3 and iTunes.

Music blogs offer a lot of useful news and information to help you keep up with the latest releases. Blogs like beatmyday.com are supported by artists like Tiësto and offer exclusive daily posts about upcoming releases, DJ mixes, and live set recordings. For a list of current blogs that cover your favorite music, search for "DJ Music Blog."

In addition, iTunes offers free podcasts from countless DJs and producers, and websites like Dubset.com have libraries of DJ sets available so you can listen to what other DJs are playing around the world. Artists like Pete Tong host radio shows that you can stream online (www.bbc.co.uk/radio1) to hear the latest and hottest new music.

Social media platforms, especially Twitter and Facebook, help you follow your favorite DJs. Many DJs post live sets, new releases and playlists. If you like the sound of a certain artist, it's also a good idea to check out other releases on the same record label.

Finally, you can use a smart phone application like Shazam to identify and discover songs you hear at clubs, online, on the radio and TV, at concerts and at retail stores. Our Shazam queue has an eclectic mix of music from dozens of different genres.

Since most DJs have access to the same music, you have to be willing to spend time curating your collection. Anyone can download the Beatport Top 100 and throw on a playlist, but a seasoned crate digger like Diplo or DJ Shadow will spend countless hours in used record stores, and even years looking for a diamond in the rough that no one else has thought to sample or mix into a set. Careful song selection and commitment to your craft, whether you're searching, shopping or mixing, are essential if you hope to develop a sound that's yours alone.

DJ Sasha: How to Establish a Unique Sound

Known for his ability to tap a crowd's emotions with his unique take on progressive music, Sasha has revolutionized the way DJs prepare and structure their sets, especially when it comes to harmonic mixing. We asked him about his history with the technique, and how it helped him form his own identifiable sound.

Sasha, how did you get started with harmonic mixing?

S: I learned to play the piano when I was a kid. I would work out the melody and I knew the keys straightaway. When I started mixing records, it sounded better when I mixed the ones that worked musically. It just became my thing.

Graeme Park and Jon Dasilva were two resident DJs at The Haçienda nightclub in Manchester, and they influenced me. I noticed that they mixed acapellas into other tracks, and it just made sense. They weren't just mixing one record into another. There was a musical flow to things. So when I started DJing myself, I had these lovely magical moments in the record booth when I was looking for that next record. I stored what works together in my brain.

Did you find the key of every track before you played it?

S: I never really memorized the keys and never worked out what they were. Some DJs sat down with a keyboard and worked out what key they were in to make these flawless sets. I never did that. I trusted my instincts and my memory. I definitely think that when you base a DJ set entirely on harmonic mixing, you can miss records sometimes. Your programming can become controlled. It's important not to let it take over. You don't want to mix records that clash, but John Digweed didn't really pay attention to harmonic mixing. He would always focus his attention on the energy of the song. His records had that kind of a clash in them, but the energy really worked, and he would put together these pulsating segments of our sets.

I would come on and play the music that would work melodically. When people send me links to old DJ sets, some of them were entirely in key, and some had really bad key clashes. It wasn't that noticeable back in the day, but people really notice it much more now. People expect that DJs should mix in key. Back in the '90s, music had such fresh energy that people didn't care so much.

Your mix CDs from the 1990s were an inspiration to a whole generation of harmonic DJs. How did you and John pick the tracks to put on them?

S: For the longest time, John and I were focused on the same type of music. We had our style that was "our sound." We would play a lot of records from each other's boxes.

To put together an album, I would sit down with my record collection for a couple of weeks, pull out records and B-sides, and find tracks that worked together. When I say worked together, I mean the keys matched. We'd just sit there with piles of records and sometimes ideas would come together quickly. Other times, it would take forever to fill that space. We'd have to find that perfect bridge. A lot of these records were not found on other DJs' mix compilations.

It was actually much easier to put these albums together— not many people made mix compilations, and music had a much longer lifespan. Today, people get bored with records so quickly. It's very hard to find records with longer time appeal.

Why is that?

S: People throw away music so quickly. When I'm looking for tracks, I go back a year and look at older music. I might think, I played this record once or twice and I loved it. It's nice to reminisce about what got you excited. For me, it's not just about the music that came out this week. If you go back in time, you will always find gems that others have missed.

There's so much music getting posted on Beatport every week that it's hard to find tracks that fit our style. What do you recommend for DJs who want to build their music collections?

S: Follow the music labels, the DJs, and the producers you love. I receive 150 promos per week, and that's after they've been filtered to fit my style. That's before I even start shopping on Beatport. There is enough music out there to create your own sound.

What makes one DJ sound different from everybody else?

S: You have to cultivate your own sound. You should remember that you're there to do a job and to deliver to the promoter and the audience. You can't be too precious about what you're doing. You have to have some flexibility and open-mindedness when it comes to your DJ sets. Once you climb the ladder, you'll get more and more flexibility in what you can play so long as the fans are there for you. There's enough music to go around to make you unique, but I also think it's difficult to define what a DJ's style really is. You'll know it when you hear it.

When I'm DJing, I often play before or after other DJs, so I don't have the whole night to myself. It's much easier to switch between DJs if you're just playing with CDs or USB sticks. With Traktor and Ableton Live in a club scenario, it's a little bit harder because you have to set up your computer. After carrying a complex setup with Ableton Live for many years with a custom controller, a large screen, and much more, it's nice to go back to the basics— and really, I recommend not getting too caught up in the technology of DJing. It has to look natural to the crowd when you perform. Nowadays, I like the simplicity.

Extra tip: Sasha backs up his music using Apple Time Machine and various external hard drives at his studio. He also carries an external drive with him. It's a useful lesson to keep in mind, because if something happens to your computer, you need to be able to restore your music quickly. We get at least ten e-mails per day from people who want to recover their Mixed In Key software after getting a new computer, so this is a common problem.

General Tips for Organizing Your Music Collection

How many times during a set have you searched through thousands of tracks in your library trying to find a particular track? The clock is ticking, and before you know it you've got less than a minute to find the perfect song.

Before the advent of MP3s, DJs would have to carefully select a cache of vinyl records—usually a full crate or two that they had to carry themselves to each gig. They were physically limited in the amount of music they could bring with them, so they often ran the risk of leaving that perfect record at home.

Today, thanks to MP3s and digital downloads, DJs can use a laptop or hard drive as a virtual crate to store thousands of records. But sorting through an avalanche of tracks presents its own set of challenges.

To start, be sure to clean up your ID3 tags. ID3 is a metadata container that stores information such as the title, artist, album, and comment in the file itself. You can edit ID3 tags using iTunes or Mixed In Key. Most audio players allow you to edit single files or even groups of them, which is often called *batch tagging*.

To edit ID3 tags inside iTunes, right-click your music file and select **Get info**. From there, you can update the song name, artist, album, genre, and album art, and you can add comments. If you import your iTunes playlists into Serato Scratch Live, Traktor, or Pioneer rekordbox software, the ID3 tag information you stored will be converted automatically.

Be sure to update key values in both the comments and key column. Having the Camelot value in both locations gives you more flexibility if you are using multiple DJ mediums (such as Traktor and Pioneer CDJs). You can keep your library organized by Camelot value and quickly identify songs that mix well together.

In addition to sorting by key, you can categorize by genre (tech house, deep house, indie, progressive house, and so on), separate new tunes from classics, or use a detailed rating system. Software like iTunes lets you easily create playlists based on the genres and ratings you identify. For more specific sorting, you can also create subgenres within a broader genre. If house is your main genre, for example, progressive or electro might be your subgenres.

Another option is to separate your music by energy level according to warm-up, peak time and last hour. You can color code tracks based on energy level as follows:

- Blue = chill/early (Level 1-4 on our scale)

- Orange = warm-up (Level 5-7)

- Red = high energy (Level 8-10)

Of course, you can also color code your tracks based on their Camelot key.

Organizing Your Digital Files

Once you've sorted your playlists in iTunes based on genre, energy level, key, or specific gig, you can import them directly into software programs such as Traktor, Serato Scratch Live, or rekordbox. If you're using a program like Traktor, make sure your software analyzes the track for BPM before you play. The analysis takes up a lot of CPU power and might cause latency (lag time) during playback, so it's better to do it at home. It's crucial to set up cue points, align beat grids, and get familiar with how your music is organized before your gig.

If you use Pioneer rekordbox, you can set hot cue and loop points, beat grids, color codes, and add all the ID3 information so it appears automatically on any CDJ-2000 display. The **Quantize** feature makes loop and cue points snap to the beat, ensuring beat-perfect loops and cues. rekordbox also enables you to export prepared tracks to a USB or SD card, and will load waveforms instantly onto the CDJ.

Organizing Your CDs

If you are burning CDs to use in CD players, we
recommend creating a separate CD for each key—for
example, put all your 8A tracks on one CD and put 9A
tracks on another. If you burn two copies of each CD, then
you can mix between songs in the same key. (And as an
added benefit, if one disc gets scratched, you can play the
other as a backup copy.)

For easy reference, print a CD label with the key code
on top (8A in this case), along with the date you made the
CD, and the full track names. Adding a Camelot key color
at the top of the label is another useful aid.

When storing CDs in a wallet for easy browsing, we
usually put 1A/1B in the front and 12A/12B in the back. It
makes intuitive sense to sort your CDs from low to high;
this way you can flip one page forward or backward to see
other harmonically compatible songs. It makes it easy to
find the next tune to play.

Preparing Your MP3s for Mixing

When people hear music, they often think louder is better. The problem is that the louder the music, the more distorted it gets. When the volume exceeds a certain level, the audio wave starts *clipping*, which results in a loss of audio quality. Turn your car radio to maximum volume and you'll hear the speakers struggling to reproduce the sound because of audio clipping.

To use a visual analogy, if you shoot a photo of deadmau5 on stage and zoom in too close, the frame might clip off his ears. The same thing happens in music when the audio signal is louder than the MP3 can handle.

In the world of DJing, it's important to play high-quality music that won't clip. You may have noticed that some files in your collection are much louder than others. It's practically guaranteed that the loudest songs will have clipping in them. All music files have a limit to how loud they can get, and many songs sold on iTunes and Beatport push this to the maximum.

Musicians and record companies apply compression and limiting in an attempt to make their recordings louder, but over-compression can cause listening fatigue, and has even been blamed for the decline of the music industry. According to mastering engineer Bob Ludwig, "When you're through listening to a whole album of this highly compressed music, your ear is fatigued. You may have enjoyed the music, but you don't really feel like going back and listening to it again."[12] A short YouTube video called "The Loudness War" (http://youtu.be/3Gmex_4hreQ) uses an audio example to explain the phenomenon.

One of the main complaints about over-compression is that it dampens the emotional impact of the music. You can avoid this problem by using software like Platinum Notes (http://www.platinumnotes.com) to adjust the volume levels of each track in your library. Platinum Notes uses studio filters to correct pitch, improve volume, and make every file ready to be played anywhere, from an iPod to a festival sound system. Similar to Mixed In Key, Platinum Notes automatically analyzes and adjusts as many files as you need.

---

[12] Earl Vickers, "The Loudness War: Background, Speculation and Recommendations," presented at the 129th Convention of the Audio Engineering Society (AES), San Francisco, California, November 4-7, 2010.
http://www.sfxmachine.com/docs/loudnesswar/loudness_war.pdf.

Interview: Mark Walker and Brian Tappert/Traxsource

Once your individual sound as a DJ has progressed significantly, chances are you'll feel creative enough to move toward producing your own tracks. We wanted to find out what happens behind the scenes in a digital DJ music store, so we talked to Mark Walker and Brian Tappert from Traxsource (www.traxsource.com) about the process of submitting music and selling it online.

Many of our readers are interested in producing. Can you talk about the process of submitting a track for sale on Traxsource?

TXS: In general terms, if the release already has a home—in the case of a remix commissioned by a label, for example—the producer will deliver it to the label via Dropbox or YouSendIt or some mode of media transfer. If the producer is still trying to shop the track—that is, find a label home for it—the most popular method to use is SoundCloud or some other streaming provider.

How long does the submission process take?

TXS: Most sites, including us, require submission of releases at least a week ahead of the date the label would like to have the release available for download.

What do you do to prepare tracks for sale?

TXS: Files are delivered to Traxsource via secure FTP and tags are created from information submitted by the content owners using our label submission system. We make music downloads available as 192 kbps and 320 kbps MP3s, as well as fully uncompressed WAV format. All the tracks we sell are DRM-free [meaning no copy protection].

We talk about the "loudness war" in *Beyond Beatmatching*. Have you seen an increase in the overall loudness of tracks submitted to the point that sound clipping is a problem?

TXS: Apart from creating the two-minute preview, encoding to MP3, and embedding the image supplied by the label or content owner, we don't alter masters in any way. We're aware of the "loudness wars," and we see evidence of it in the tracks we receive, but everything sold is an exact digital copy of the masters provided by the record companies.

Preparing for a Live Set

Like any live performance, putting on your game face for any DJ set should be not just a routine, but a ritual. Mixing music is obviously your primary task, but proper preparation can help your set go much more smoothly. The first step is to do as much research as possible ahead of time about the vibe of the venue you're playing. You might need to adapt your personal style in a way that best matches the venue, but don't go overboard; if you're good enough to have landed the gig in the first place, then you've already got some clout going in.

As you prepare for each venue, think about what type of crowd will be there and how long they'll stay. Try to picture the flow of the night. When does the energy need to pick up? When is the peak time of the evening?

You can approach controlling the energy level in a few different ways. One way is to slowly build the energy throughout the night to a peak level, then dip briefly at the end. If you play mainstream music, another option is to rotate genres, spending 30 minutes per genre. The best way to be prepared for any type of set is to create a music management system that works for you.

Proper preparation for a weekend gig should begin early in the week. David Mancuso, who got his start in New York back in 1970 as the DJ for his own roving party called The Loft, remembers that most of the week revolved around preparations for the next gig. "I found out that if I started working on Thursday I would be in too much of a rush, so I began to get ready from high noon on Wednesday. My diet, my sleep, the sound, the balloons, the menu, the floor, the theme—everything built up to Saturday night."[13]

---

[13] Tim Lawrence. *Love Saves the Day: A History of American Dance Music Culture, 1970-1979* (Durham, NC: Duke University Press, 2004), 23-24.

7. Create Your Own Mashups

There are a few more ways you can differentiate your sound, even when you're playing the same tracks as another DJ. One way is to create a mashup.

At its most basic, a mashup blends two songs together to create a new one, but there's really no limit to the number of sampled elements it can contain. Probably the most well-known (and controversial) mashup ever made was Danger Mouse's *The Grey Album*, which mashed the solo vocals from Jay-Z's *The Black Album* together with digitally chopped selections of Beatles songs from their classic *White Album*. It was a work of genius, and needless to say, when it leaked online in 2004, it also stirred up a lot of legal questions about sampling, rights ownership and copyright control.

Of course, there's also a not-so-fine line that separates a mashup as masterful as *The Grey Album* from a cheap, cheesy knockoff. Mixing five huge dance anthems together might energize a crowd, but to a lot of devoted fans of dance music, it degrades the clubbing experience. Even worse, you might piss off the club manager, which means you've lost any chance of coming back. Mashups can be powerful, but it's best to use them in moderation. With that warning in mind, there are a number of ways to make them.

You can use your DJ mixing setup to produce a mashup live in a club, or you can use software tools like Ableton Live, Logic, Cubase, or Mixed In Key Mashup to make one ahead of time and save it as an MP3. Whatever method you choose, keep in mind that the most common (and accessible) mashups take the beat from one song and the vocals from another. A more complex mashup might alternate between two different melodies while using an acapella from a third song.

If they're done well, mashups can fundamentally change how people remember songs. Like *The Grey Album*, they can even become just as famous (or more so) than the original songs. Two mashups of tracks by David Guetta and LMFAO are perfect examples. Guetta's production partner Joachim Garraud took the lead vocal of Guetta's "Love Don't Let Me Go" and mixed it with The Egg's "Walking Away (Tocadisco Remix)." The result made a huge splash on YouTube and was a worldwide club hit. A few years later, DJ Inphinity's mashup of LMFAO's vocals over Chuckie's "Let the Bass Kick" became one of the biggest summer anthems of 2009.

The best mashups usually don't go for too much complexity, but there's still an art to making the different elements mesh together smoothly. Let's take a look at Kaskade's "Move for First Aid" as an example.

The mashup blends the following tracks:

Michael Woods, "First Aid"
Camelot key: 4A
Kaskade and deadmau5, "Move for Me" (acapella)
Camelot key: 4A

As you can see, both of the original songs are harmonically compatible. When you're mixing in a club, chances are you're changing the key with practically every mix. It's common to mix from 8A into 7A into 6A in just minutes. But when you're making a mashup, it's usually best to choose two songs in the same key to make things easier on yourself.

It's also important to be aware of key changes that already exist within a song. Even if two songs are in 4A, the chorus of one might be in a different key, so it's possible you won't be able to overlay them without dissonance. When you're creating a mashup, make sure the specific sections of the tunes you blend together are in the same key—or harmonically related keys, if you have time to experiment.

DJ Prince: Guru of Harmonic Mixing

DJ Prince has been our mentor for all things related to DJing as a musical art form. We spoke to him about his approach to making mashups and mixing harmonically.

You launched one of the world's first websites about harmonic mixing back in 1996. When did you start using the technique yourself?

P: I guess I started out mixing in harmony around 1987, at first just by accident. At that time, I had to concentrate really hard to keep the beats in sync, and when the songs coincidentally were in the same key or in harmony, I had a hard time hearing which song was going faster or which one was going slower. I guess they blended so well that it was hard to tell them apart. It puzzled me why this happened now and again.

Another factor was the club and DJ magazine *Mix Mag*. It used to review the DJ battle sets for DMC's World Mixing Championship eliminations in the UK, and it used the phrase "out of key." Curious as I was, I had to investigate what this key thing was all about. There was no Internet to Google the information, and no harmonic mixing gurus were around, so I did it the old-fashioned way: I went to an actual library—you know, where they have books and everybody whispers. I spent hours and hours reading about music theory, although I couldn't play a single note on an instrument. What I really found useful were these notation books of pop songs; *Pop Hits of 88* was one of them. I remember you could find the root key at the start of each notation. I wrote down the root key of all the songs I could find and tried to mix them. Then I had a eureka moment: This actually works!

I always had an ear for what sounded good and what didn't. I just couldn't explain it until then. I was so excited; it was like finding the holy grail of mixing. On the other side of the Atlantic [from Norway, where I live], they had discovered it long before me. I was somewhat disappointed and extremely happy when I found the DJ magazine called *Harmonic Mixing* by Mark Davis. After reading that, it all made sense. The harmonic overlay chart was first printed there. I had seen the content before, only as the circle of fifths, but I didn't make the connection at the time. When the *UK Mix Mag Update*, a kind of weekly newspaper for DJs, listed the top 100 club hits along with their BPM and keys, I was hooked!

You helped thousands of DJs discover harmonic mixing before Mixed In Key and other websites came along. Why do you think so many people are interested in this technique?

P: People are often very passionate about their art or hobby, and they go to extreme measures to perfect their skills. Some focus on beatmatching and some on scratching, while others just want to DJ and make the floor rock. And then there are the "nerds" or the perfectionists: they always want to push their talent a little farther than the rest. Mixing harmonically actually makes perfect sense, and it is the right thing to do—not just for the studio/mega-mixing DJs, but also for live DJs. Though harmonic mixing makes a mix sound good, it actually does have another function. It has a psychological effect on the dance floor. God truly is a DJ when he can manipulate the feeling and take people on a journey using his harmonic mixing skills. I guess more and more DJs became aware of this and were interested to learn more. I was one of them. That's why I focused on teaching others through my website back in the early days of the Internet. Of course, another reason is that all those masters of mixing at that time (Ben Liebrand, for instance) were a huge influence on up-and-coming DJs.

Before the technology came along, what was the typical process for DJs to get their tracks keyed for DJing?

P: We either asked a musical friend to help us, or we tried to do it ourselves using a keyboard and a good pair of ears. There were professional services around, like Camelot, providing the keys and BPM, but it cost a lot for up-and-coming DJs.

If you did it yourself, it took some time, right?

P: The actual process of finding the key was time-consuming if you didn't have perfect pitch. Many have relative pitch hearing, but a lot of DJs are completely tone deaf—still, they're eager to learn. It's actually possible to learn to get a better ear for harmonic mixing just by training. I used to have a Korg Poly-800 synthesizer. This was my best friend. I spent hundreds, if not thousands, of hours keying songs on it. First, I tried to find the root key. I closed my eyes and tried to listen for the note that blended seamlessly with the song playing. After I found the root key, I had to determine whether it was in a major or minor chord. In the beginning, the whole process could take up to 20 minutes for each song. It was a good way to learn how to play the keyboard, much to my family's frustration.

In recent years, mashups have become much more common. We heard a story about you and Norwegian television.

P: Well, it's a kind of an ironic and tragic story. It started at Spellemansprisen, which is the Norwegian version of the Grammys. Yosef Wolde-Mariam and Tshawe Baqwa from Madcon, who are both of African origin, were presenting the grand prize, "Song of the Year." [Madcon is one of Norway's biggest rap/pop duos.] The winner was the hillbilly band Plumbo for its song "Møkkamann," which directly translates as "shitman." When the members of Plumbo went on stage, they were high on winning the grand prize and maybe a little drunk. Their lead singer, Lars Erik Blokkhus, took the microphone and said to Madcon: "When I look at you two, this song gets a new name: 'Moccaman.'" In this case, he used "mocca" to refer to "dark" coffee beans, and it was obviously a bad joke. The crowd started to boo and throw stuff on stage. The singer from Plumbo was quick to apologize, but later Tshawe from Madcon called him a bad word, and a member from another band poured beer over Plumbo's lead singer on live TV. The scandal was all over the news. Twitter and Facebook exploded with discussions and arguments.

When I woke up the next day, I was bombarded with this story. All my friends online were discussing who was right and who was wrong. It was overwhelming. I was actually getting tired of all the news coverage and came up with a cunning plan. What if Plumbo and Madcon straightened out their differences, became friends, and made a song together? So I took "Møkkamann" and mashed it up with Madcon's "Beggin'." The songs were in D minor, and some parts sounded really good together. It's not my finest or most technically brilliant mashup, but it sure was a fantastic idea, politically and timing-wise. It took me about 20 minutes to make it. Then I uploaded it to a streaming service and shared the link on my Facebook page. After that, it just exploded.

It had 50,000 hits within two days, and I was all over the media with headlines like "DJ with a reconciliation song," "DJ wants Plumbo and Madcon to be friends," "DJ Prince could be the DJ for the United Nations' Conflict Department," and the list goes on. Radio stations picked it up. This was the first time one of my mashups created such a media storm and so much hype, which is kind of nice. I think Plumbo and Madcon are friends now, but I don't think they will ever make a song together.

Should DJs experiment with making mashups themselves?

P: Creating a mashup that fits together well is actually a very rewarding experience. It is like a composer discovering a great melody, a photographer finding the right inspiration, or a scientist making a breakthrough. All the songs of the world are like pieces of a puzzle, so when two parts fit, it gives us pleasure and enjoyment. It's also a natural process for DJs to play around with mixing songs together, and some mixes are good as mashups. Unfortunately, most mashups aren't endorsed by the record companies, and some DJs have had their YouTube account deleted (me, for instance) or have faced prosecution (like mashup artist Girl Talk). All in all, everything is a mashup or inspiration, but that's a topic for another book, I guess. I say be creative; it's your right. Share your mashups, but don't sell them. And *please* mix in harmony. If the mashup is good enough, who knows? Maybe it will get an official release, endorsed by the record companies, and take you to stardom. I'll be listening!

An Easy Way to Make Mashups

We always try to stay attuned to the demands of the DJs we work with, and one thing we discovered was that a user-friendly software solution for mashups didn't really exist. We wanted to be able create mashups in five minutes or less, but there was no easy way to do it. That was the inspiration for our cleverly named Mashup software.

This is the audio editor that we always wanted for Windows and Mac because it's so easy to use. All you have to do is drag music files from iTunes or your hard drive into the Mashup browser, and the software automatically detects which files are most compatible. A value of 100 means the mashup will be harmonic, while a value of 0 means it will be dissonant. You can add as many tracks as you want, and even create a mixtape from 20 different songs.

We designed Mashup to beatmatch tracks automatically, and simplify the process of adjusting tempo, editing volume envelopes and tweaking phasing, so you can render a new audio file in a matter of minutes (check out http://Mashup.MixedInKey.com for a tutorial and digital download). It makes the mashup process easier, but remember, like any software program, this is just a tool. Mashups can be a great outlet for asserting your creativity as a DJ and a producer, but there are also plenty of other great ways to boost your DJ skills. Once again, it circles back to *energy*.

8. Use Advanced Harmonic Mixing Techniques

When you really start to dig into the more specialized secrets of modern DJing, a whole new dimension of creativity reveals itself. We can't say it enough, because it bears repeating: DJing isn't just about playing records anymore; it's a *musical* art form that requires hard work, dedication and a keen ear for new "chops" to add to your repertoire. You can't be a true musician if you don't have chops.

David Guetta brought this point home to us by describing a technique that he had been using himself for a long time; we couldn't believe that we'd never thought of it. Remember back in Chapter 2 when we discussed dissonance (clashing keys in a harmonic mix) as something to avoid? Well, that's not always the case.

Mixing in Related Keys

Without getting into the details of music theory (which you can research on your own), it's true that any musical key you choose on the Camelot Wheel shares a special harmonic relationship with certain other keys. There are other key combinations that work outside the harmonically compatible group (i.e., 5A > 4A / 5B / 6A) we described in Chapter 2.

Guetta mentioned a technique that translates into the following: You can add four to your current Camelot code and get some unusual and compelling results. So if you mix from 10B into 2B, it sounds dissonant at first, but sometimes it *works*.

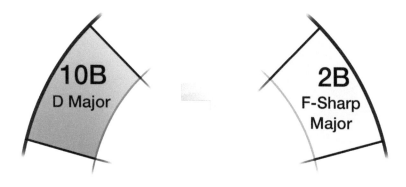

It's not always compatible, so you have to experiment with individual songs before you bring it into a set, but some songs will sound insanely cool when you mix them like this. Tracks with simple melodies usually yield the best results; if they're too complex, your mix can go off the rails.

Another interesting trick is to mix diagonally on the Camelot Wheel from 8B into 9A or from 9A into 8B. This sounds great because the individual notes of the two keys are harmonically related. You can extrapolate this technique to any key, adding one to the Camelot key if going from B to A (5B > 6A), or subtracting one if going from A to B (8A > 7B).

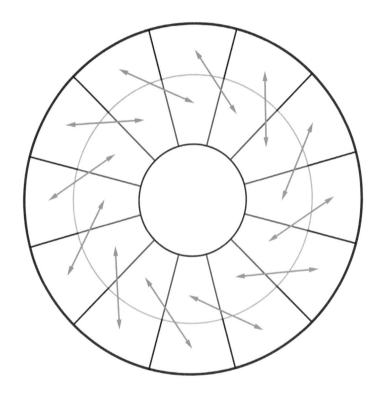

So if we can go from 8B to 9A, why can't we go from 8B to 7A? The scales of 8B and 7A contain dissonant intervals, so the mix wouldn't work harmonically.

Again, it's important to keep in mind that mixing harmonically takes a bit of preparation before your gig. As we discussed in Chapter 2, once you've labeled your tracks using the Camelot code, you can move quickly from one song to the next by simply glancing at the key code. But moving around the Camelot Wheel to do harmonically *related* mixes, like the ones we're suggesting here, takes practice.

Energy Boost Mixing

If you want to give your dance floor a quick burst of excitement at any point in your set, an energy-boosting mix is the way to do it. This happens when you mix into a key that is one or two semitones *higher* than your current key. For example, if you are in C minor, your next key should be D-flat major (one semitone), or D minor (two semitones, or one whole tone). Going from C to D (two semitones) is the best mix.

This is more commonly referred to among musicians as *modulating keys*, and has been in use for decades in a lot of pop music. (It chills our hearts to say it, but Barry Manilow and Celine Dion are probably the biggest proponents of key modulation; you usually hear it toward the end of one of their songs, when the key keeps changing and the melody seems to be "climbing.")

To go up one semitone using the Camelot Wheel, just add seven to the number of your current track. For example, if you're playing a song in E-flat minor (2A), you'll need to mix it into a song in E minor (9A). To go up two semitones, just add two to your current Camelot number, so if you're in C minor (5A), add two and you'll get D minor (7A). When you play your next tune in 7A, you'll experience an energy-boost mix.

Obviously, the effect increases when you double the boost. For example, start with a song in 2A and listen closely to the melody and overall feel of the song. Then mix into a song in 4A (a two-semitone jump), and note how it sounds. The figure below visualizes the effect. When you use an energy boost, you're always moving to the right on a piano keyboard.

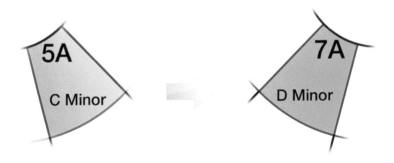

The rule is always the same and will work with any key, and the effect on the dance floor is immediate. Your audience will subconsciously note the lift and will generally respond positively to the boost. But again, as with mixing in related keys, the technique may not work with every song, so practicing beforehand is essential. Jumping two semitones tends to be a bit safer than a one-semitone mix, but both will work well if you manage your mix with your ears open.

Of course, like anything that feels good, it's always best to use energy boost mixing in moderation, or you risk lessening the desired effect on your audience. As we've said before, the main thing is to stay tuned in to what's happening on the dance floor. If it's already packed and moving, just keep going strong without changing your plan.

Intuitively, you might think that mixing in the opposite direction of an energy boost will slow down the dance floor, and you're right. If you're getting toward the end of the night, a move counter-clockwise on the Camelot Wheel to a song that's two key codes lower than what you're playing can send the signal that your set is winding to a close. Your audience will get the idea.

As a rule, we don't recommend trying an energy drop like this in the middle of your set until you're well-acquainted with the possible results. Even so, there are times when this effect can give your mix some great contrast and turn the focus of your audience right back on you. It's an attention-grabber, and if it gets people talking about your set in a positive way, it'll get you more gigs.

One last tip: it's also better to mix a boost quickly because the melodies will clash. You're going for a specific effect and not a long blend. If you do it just once in a while, the technique adds a quirky degree of complexity and contrast to your set because it violates the rules of harmonic mixing. But again, be careful not to overdo it.

Harmonic Scratching: Is It Possible, and Should You Do It?

If you've never tried scratching, give it a shot just to see what it feels like. It's not a skill that most DJs can just pick up; it takes practice and refinement to reach a point where you can feel comfortable doing it. Scratching is all about approaching the turntable as an instrument—in fact, this is how the term "turntablism" originated.

Any turntable, CDJ, or digital controller with a turntable-like interface allows DJs to scratch. There are more than 60 different scratch techniques—chirp, crab, flare, transforming and beat-juggling are just a few—so if you want to explore the technique in depth, there's plenty of room for you to stretch out creatively.

For our purposes though, we want to take a look at how you might incorporate scratching into your club set. Most dance music DJs tend to veer away from scratching because it involves dexterity and skill set that differs radically from mixing—but also because there's a

perception that extended scratching routines will sound
out-of-place in a club environment.

According to DJ A-Trak, nothing could be further from
the truth. If it's done with taste and attention to detail, a
well-timed scratch routine can energize a dance floor. In
remembering his friend Adam Goldstein (aka DJ AM),
who always supported innovation in DJing, A-Trak wrote a
moving blog post that summed up his thoughts about what
was appropriate for a club.

"When I played more commercial clubs I used to hold
back on the turntablism," A-Trak wrote. "But whenever
[Adam] was there, he relentlessly urged me to do a routine.
I mean, he pushed me until I had to do it! He would grab

the mic and tell the crowd 'A-Trak didn't want to do a routine but I'm forcing him, you guys need to see this,' and really got them psyched. Then he'd do air scratches during my juggles."

From the standpoint of harmonic mixing, if you cue up a small sample and hit the play button on the beat, it sounds cool as long as it's in the same key as the song you're playing. It could be a conga loop, a horn melody, a drumbeat, spoken word, or a line from another song; the main thing, as we stress throughout this book, is to be *musical*. Scratching may not always sound like it has a harmonic element, but veteran hip-hop DJs like Grand Mixer DXT understand that the technique can evoke notes and pitches, just like you can with a keyboard.

If you listen to DXT's scratches on the Herbie Hancock classic "Rockit," for example, you get the idea. "That was completely from a musical foundation," DXT says. "I was thinking of sax solos, or scatting like Ella Fitzgerald. I wasn't sure if I could actually make that happen on a turntable, but just in trying, the mechanics came to help me physically move my hands and the mixer and the turntable in a way where what I was hearing in my head came out on the decks. Musicians work that way too."[14]

---

[14] Bill Murphy. "Breakin' In," *Remix* magazine (July 2004), 114.

When we asked A-Trak about how much time you should take for a scratch routine in a club, he recommended keeping it short—two minutes at the most. "Shorter routines may not showcase your talent," he said, "but longer routines may lose people who just came out to go clubbing."

As with every technique you absorb into your repertoire, the key is to experiment and find what routine length works for you.

Interview with DJ Enferno: Turning the Tables

DJ Enferno has made a name for himself as Madonna's DJ, but he's also an accomplished producer and the 2003 U.S. champion of the DMC World DJ Championships. He definitely knows a thing or two about scratching, and has made a career out of tastefully merging elements of turntablism into his sets.

How did winning the U.S. championship in 2003 affect your career?

E: Winning the DMC title was a dream come true for me as a turntablist and as a DJ. After that, I started getting my first bookings to perform outside of my own city, Washington, D.C. That was a big step for me. But to be honest, most people in the club world aren't familiar with the DMC. I've had to keep pushing the envelope creatively with my music and my Live Remix Project, which is the primary reason for my success today.

What role should scratching play as part of a live set? How often do you do it?

E: Scratching isn't necessary to be a good DJ. Remember, DJing and turntablism aren't the same thing. Scratching goes along with turntablism, which is performing with turntables as instruments. DJing is the art of entertaining a crowd through song selection. During my DJ sets, I only scratch a little bit, depending on what type of venue I'm performing in. If the crowd is watching and wants to be entertained, then I'll scratch more. It's really important not to overdo it. When people want to dance, they usually don't want to hear someone scratching all night.

Now, if I'm performing my Live Remix sets, then that's a different story. Those are completely performance-based, where I play and sample keyboards and turntables to create music. Scratching during a Live Remix set is a must. After I get a feel for the crowd—and if they're into it—I definitely show off a little.

Scratching was one of the pillars of the hip-hop movement. Some of the young guys coming up today have a sense that it's an old-school technique. Does it work well with digital DJing?

E: I think it works great in the digital DJ world, if the DJ is good at it and has the discipline and the experience to do it at the right time. Just about all the big scratch DJs that I used to look up to (and still do actually), like Craze and A-Trak, all use digital DJ systems.

What's the best way to learn scratching? What do you recommend?

E: The best way is to make friends with someone who knows how to scratch and have that person teach you. Most people don't have this option. I recommend going on YouTube and searching for tutorials. There are tons of them there that I wish I had access to when I was learning. If you really want in-depth training, you can even sign up for DJ Q-Bert's Skratch University.

You never know who's in the audience, right? We heard that Madonna's music director discovered you by going to your gig.

E: Yeah, Kevin Antunes saw me at a gig in his hometown, Orlando. I was performing an all-Live Remix set, and he tracked me down and called me the next day to talk about the tour and see whether I was interested in being considered. You can imagine my answer to that question.

What's it like to work as a DJ on stage with a live band?

E: It's definitely a different experience than working the usual nightclub circuit. I play a part in a show to support the artist, as opposed to being the featured performer. The audiences were huge, and the shows were frequent. Traveling to so many different cities in a short period of time sometimes left me wondering what city I was in when I woke up in the morning. I loved being around so many talented people, and I think I grew as an artist and performer by being in such a group. I'll never forget the first big show and being in front of 50,000 people.

Message from the authors: You're about half-way done. Please tell your friends about this book! Thank you very much. –Your authors, Yakov and Eric

9. Build the Perfect DJ Laptop

DJing has come a long way from just two turntables and a mixer. For one thing, the practical hassle of hauling crates full of vinyl to a club is no longer a concern (unless you *want* to spin real vinyl—and Serato makes even that possible, without the heavy lifting). But more importantly, DJs can now live, work and travel with their entire mix/production studio on just a laptop, and that's something revolutionary.

Looking back, it's easy to see that when everything went digital, the gradual advances in technology literally changed the face of popular music, resulting in an explosion of remixes, mashups, mixtapes, and entirely new musical styles like glitch, grime and dubstep. On top of that, programs like Ableton Live, Serato and Traktor democratized the art of DJing, making it more accessible to more people so that anyone with a disc drive and a dream could climb on board.

But as any professional DJ knows, it's not just about the tools you have; it's what you *do* with them that counts. We're obviously huge fans of technology, but we also advocate learning how to use every available method of DJing, from old-school to nu-school, so that you're well-rounded and prepared to DJ in any situation. If you show up to a club that only has turntables or a pair of CDJs, you should be ready to play.

That said, this chapter is all about helping you put together a DJ setup that's right for you.

Getting Started

If you're new to DJing—and even if you're upgrading to a new system—we recommend the simplest setup possible. Start with a minimalist approach and set out to do as much as you can with a minimum of equipment (such as one MacBook Pro and a MIDI controller, or two CDJs and a mixer). You should choose the setup that's most comfortable for you, but again, be flexible enough to adapt to any equipment so you're prepared to play at any venue.

Whether you prefer to use turntables, CDs, or a MIDI controller, digital options are always available. The list of DJ software applications is constantly growing, but based on what we've seen from thousands of DJs who use Mixed In Key, we've noticed that the most popular options are Serato Scratch Live, Native Instruments Traktor, Pioneer rekordbox, and Ableton Live.

At the risk of over-generalizing (and we certainly don't mean to offend anyone), we've come up with a few basic ways for you to determine what kind of DJ you are:

- If you like simplicity and want the feel of vinyl, go with **Serato**. Keep in mind that Serato is a closed-box system and needs compatible hardware to run.

- If you switch constantly between songs, don't mind turning a lot of knobs, and consider yourself a tech geek, choose **Ableton Live**. Live blurs the line between DJing and production, but it also requires a lot more preparation before each gig.

- If you prefer a software package that's sleek and stylish with a lot of functionality and customization options, choose **Traktor**. Traktor is easy to use out of the box, and can work with controllers, turntables, or CDJs.

- If you like using CDs or want the ease of showing up at a club with only a USB full of prepared music, choose **Pioneer rekordbox**. rekordbox has added a digital element to CDJ DJing, enabling more pre-show preparation options.

All four of these options are valid and have benefits, so you really can't go wrong. If you can, try them all before you choose what works best for you.

How to Build the Best MacBook for DJing

Apple's MacBook Pro has become the most popular laptop among professional DJs, and for good reason. The machine is sleek, fast and durable, with a beautiful high-resolution screen that's rarely a strain on your eyes.

The one drawback is that MacBooks are expensive, but if you're on a budget, there are a few loopholes you can exploit to make your new laptop more affordable. The secret is to focus on the individual parts of the computer that are essential to DJing and music production.

The first thing to keep in mind is that every laptop is made with parts manufactured by different companies. Even though the MacBook is designed by Apple in California, it's assembled in China with a variety of different parts.

At the heart of every laptop is the CPU. There are only two companies in the world that make them: Intel and

AMD. In 2012, if you buy a CPU on Amazon, you'll pay usually between $150 and $200. Laptop manufacturers usually negotiate a sweeter deal with Intel, but ultimately it's still the same product you can buy yourself. When you configure your laptop, most companies will offer a selection of CPUs, as follows:

- 2.4GHz dual-core Intel Core i5

- 2.8GHz dual-core Intel Core i7

- 2.2GHz quad-core Intel Core i7

- 2.4GHz quad-core Intel Core i7

Most people have no idea what this information means. Basically, all you need to know is that quad (meaning "four") is twice as fast as dual (meaning "two"). When you see a value like "2.4GHz," it's telling you how fast your computer can execute instructions—decode files, create MP3s, and so on. When Apple tells you that your computer has a 2.4GHz dual-core CPU, this means that the machine has two identical "brains," and each brain has the ability to perform 2.4 billion calculations per second. A quad-core computer, with its four brains, is twice as fast. This is why a quad-core CPU costs more, but we still recommend getting the least expensive quad-core you can find—it'll be plenty fast.

Memory is another key component to look at. Most MacBooks come with four gigabytes of random access memory (RAM), which is what allows Traktor, Ableton Live and other programs to load projects without slowing down. The good thing is that memory is cheap, and the more you add, the better your computer will perform. In 2012, if you upgrade Apple's standard allocation of RAM from 4GB to 8GB, it will cost you an extra $200. According to our research, the same memory can be ordered from Amazon for less than $50. You could upgrade it yourself, but it's important that your MacBook has 8GB either way.

Hard drives can be mechanical or solid state. Mechanical hard drives have moving parts inside, like an old clock. Solid state hard drives are like a giant version of a digital camera's memory card—a little stick that contains a lot of data. As you might imagine, solid state technology leaves mechanical technology in the dust.

The bottom two performers are the fastest mechanical hard drives in the world. Every solid state drive beats them:

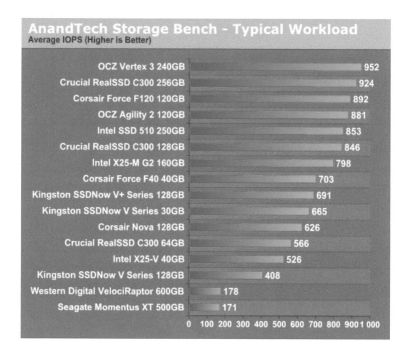

With a solid state drive, your applications will load faster, and your laptop will wake up from sleep mode almost instantly. Naturally, we recommend getting a solid state drive—it's the single best improvement you can make to the overall speed of your computer.

The one down side of solid state is the price. Apple's own configuration specs list a 128GB solid state hard drive for $200, but if you want to double the size to 256GB, the price *triples* to a whopping $600. If the prospect of paying that kind of money for a hard drive makes you wince, here's what you can do: hack your own.

Remember, Apple assembles its laptops from different parts, so the exact same hard drive that Apple wants to sell you is available on Amazon for half the price. In 2012, you can get a fantastic 256GB solid state drive with a 3-year warranty for $300.

We recommend buying your MacBook from Apple with the cheapest 500GB mechanical hard drive, and then choosing a solid state drive and installing it yourself (according to Apple, this will not void the MacBook's warranty). A do-it-yourself manual that shows you how to choose the right part and reconfigure your MacBook can be downloaded here:
http://manuals.info.apple.com/en_US/MBPRO_13inch_Mid2009_Hard_Drive_DIY.pdf.

Finally, you need to choose a display. Apple's Glossy version looks very shiny and has the disadvantage of reflecting light in bright conditions, no matter where you are. The Matte version looks professional, and it's easy to read under any light conditions—you can use it outdoors in bright sunshine, and it won't reflect a thing. A Matte display costs an extra $150, but again, it's worth it.

If the laptop we describe here puts you over budget, you can shop for a Windows 7 laptop using this guide. Since MacBooks run on the same Intel CPUs and the same solid state drives that are available for Windows, you can get a great Windows laptop with the *exact* same hardware for a lower price.

If your heart is still set on a MacBook Pro, you can strip away some options. You can downgrade to 4GB of RAM and still run most DJ software; even Ableton Live should run smoothly, unless you're creating complex projects. By the same token, you can also choose a slower CPU; a dual-core model will still work well for many projects.

If your budget is really tight, you can scale back to the MacBook's standard Glossy display, but for reasons stated above, we can't recommend scaling back to a mechanical hard drive—the differences are just too great. At the very least, a solid state hard drive needs to be your top priority when building your MacBook.

To save even more, you can also consider buying a refurbished MacBook directly from Apple. These are posted online at the Apple Store (scroll down to the lower left of the home page and click on **Special Deals**) but they tend to get snatched up quickly, so you'll need to check in often to get a jump on other potential buyers.

Headphones

Even though many DJs treat them as an afterthought, headphones are one of the most important pieces of your DJ setup. Find a comfortable pair of closed-back headphones that don't hurt your ears after you've worn them for a half-hour or more. With this in mind, you should buy from a store that accepts returns if you don't think the headphones are 100% comfortable.

Custom Earplugs

If you're going to spend multiple nights each week listening to loud music, we strongly recommend custom earplugs. You only have one set of ears, and hearing loss is irreversible. These earplugs can be expensive because they're shaped to fit your ear, but the bonus is they maintain sound quality while reducing the decibel level. Companies like Etymotic will take an impression of your ear cavity to make an earplug that fits your ear perfectly.[15] We've used many custom earplugs over the years, so here's the most basic advice: a Google search for "hearing aid

---

[15] "High-Fidelity Hearing Protection," accessed January 30, 2012. http://www.etymotic.com/hp/erme.html.

near (your zip code)" should turn up some options near where you live. It's typically a lab that caters to people with hearing loss, but they are happy to accommodate a musician or a DJ.

Soundcards

An external soundcard makes your audio sound clean, speeds up your laptop's processing power, and provides system stability. Some DJ controllers or other hardware such as the Pioneer CDJ-2000 include a built-in soundcard. Check your manufacturer's guide if you think you already have one.

If you don't own a stand-alone soundcard yet, look for a USB version in any DJ store. Native Instruments makes excellent soundcards, but there are plenty of other options.

Minimal latency is required for accurate manipulation, and multiple channels are usually required for sending audio to external equipment and for monitoring. Serato and Traktor products include a proprietary audio interface; you'll need to research appropriate interfaces for other DJ software applications.

Since technology changes so fast, for our purposes here it doesn't make sense to get into detailed descriptions of what each soundcard can do. Our advice instead is to visit a DJ technology blog like DigitalDJTips.com or

DJTechTools.com, and look for reviews of soundcards in their archives. You'll get great information directly from people we trust.

Back Up Your Music Files

We have a unique perspective on data backups because we sell digital software. Many people email us with requests to download Mixed In Key again because their computer has crashed or was stolen. We always help, but we also feel the pain. It's bad enough to lose your computer; it's devastating to lose your work. The best thing you can do is to routinely back up your data, and keep it in a safe place (such as an external hard drive or backup computer) where it won't be lost in case something happens to your laptop.

As Sasha told us (see Chapter 6), he keeps external hard drives all over his studio. He also uses Apple's Time Machine backup utility, and carries an external hard drive with him wherever he goes. Sasha's ability to restore his music means he's ready to play no matter what happens.

The Live Performance Rescue Plan

No matter how much you've prepared for a show, epic failures are always a possibility. Experienced DJs have told us plenty of horror stories about spilled drinks on laptops, overloaded power outlets in the DJ booth, and much worse. Whatever happens, the last thing you want to do is panic.

It's always a good idea to burn two DJ mixes to CDs in advance. One should be a lounge mix that you can play early in the night, and the other should be a peak-time mix in case things go wrong at 1:00 in the morning. Bring both discs to every gig, so if you run into an equipment problem, you can play a mix over the club's PA and keep the show going while you deal with the issue.

If your laptop crashes but you have CDJs available, it's also smart to bring a USB drive loaded with the same two mixes, along with the unmixed tracks. This allows you to keep mixing from the USB stick while you address the problem.

It's a rite of passage for a DJ to experience an equipment failure in front of a live audience. Having a rescue plan means that your audience may not even realize that something went wrong.

10. Mix a Flawless DJ Set

We all have our favorite songs, movies, books and live performances—but what makes a DJ mix memorable? A great DJ set can *connect* you with something larger than yourself, whether it's the surging crowd on a packed dance floor or the churning, emotive power of a well-juiced mix.

If you've ever made a mixtape for someone, you know what it means to create a mood, tell a story, or stir a memory with the music you choose. This has been a part of modern DJing since the beginning, from Kool Herc's block parties in the Bronx to Larry Levan's epic sets at the Paradise Garage in downtown Manhattan. DJ Steve D'Acquisto, who was Francis Grasso's apprentice in the early 1970s, consciously played with the *language* of the music he was spinning.

"[Steve] wasn't a mixer," Frankie Knuckles recalled, "but back then mixing wasn't that important. His selection of music was excellent, and he kept the energy going. With him it was all about the words. He would actually match up the words between one song and another so that they would form a complete sentence."[16]

---

[16] Tim Lawrence. *Love Saves the Day: A History of American Dance Music Culture, 1970-1979* (Durham, NC: Duke University Press, 2004), 62.

This is where the *art* of making a great mix comes in. What songs you choose, and how you choose to mix them, will determine how much of a lasting impression you leave with your audience.

Kaskade: How to Make a Great Harmonic Mix

Let's examine the flow of an artfully crafted harmonic DJ set. We've mentioned Kaskade's "BBC Radio 1 Essential Mix"[17] before, and we think it's a prime example of harmonic mixing at its finest. All the song transitions and mashups were created with harmonic compatibility in mind.

---

[17] "Kaskade's BBC Radio 1 Essential Mix," SoundCloud. Accessed January 30, 2012. http://soundcloud.com/kaskade/kaskades-bbc-radio-1-essential.

Here's a look at the playlist, with Camelot keys attached:

1. Kaskade and Adam K – "Raining" (Intro Mix) – 7A

2. Kaskade – "Eyes" – 8A/8B

3. Tiësto and Hardwell – "Zero 76" – 8A

4. Kaskade – "Angel on My Shoulder" (EDX Mix) – 8A

5. R3hab and Swanky Tunes – "Sendin My Love" (Kaskade Mix) – 8A

6. Kaskade – "Dynasty" (Dada Life Mix) – 7A/10B

7. Tommy Trash – "The End" – 7A

8. Nicky Romero – "Solar" – 7A

9. Kaskade – "Empty Streets" (Acapella) – 7A/8A

10. Dimitri Vegas and Like Mike with Dada Life – "Tomorrow" (Digital Lab and Pedro Henriques Dub) – 6A

11. Kaskade – "Stars Align" (Acapella) – 6A

12. Skylar Grey – "Invisible" (Kaskade Mix) – 5A/5B

13. Michael Woods – "First Aid" – 4A

14. Kaskade and deadmau5 – "Move for Me" (Acapella) – 4A

15. Kaskade with Rebecca and Fiona – "Turn It Down" – 4A

16. Boy Lost – "Itza Trumpet Thing" (Mind Electric Mix) – 3A

17. Fedde Le Grand – "So Much Love" – 2A

18. Laidback Luke – "Natural Disaster" (Instrumental) – 1A

19. Kaskade – "All That You Give" (Acapella) – 1A

20. David Guetta and Avicii – "Sunshine" – 12A

21. Sebastian Ingrosso and Alesso – "Calling" – 12B

22. Alex Gaudino – "Kissed" – 11A

23. Kaskade and EDX – "Don't Stop Dancing" (Acapella) – 11B

24. Wolfgang Gartner – "Undertaker" – 10A

25. Kaskade – "Steppin' Out" (Acapella) – 10B

26. James Blunt – "Dangerous" (Deniz Koyu and Johan Wedel Mix) – 11A

27. Coldplay – "Every Teardrop Is a Waterfall" (SHM Mix) – 11B

28. Dirty South and Thomas Gold – "Alive" – 11A

29. DBN and Menck – "Redemption" (Instrumental Mix) – 9A/9B

30. Kaskade – "Step One Two" (Acapella) – 9A/9B

31. Kaskade – "It's You It's Me" (Dance.Love Mix) – 9B

32. Calvin Harris – "Feel So Close" – 9B

33. Switchfoot – "Always Yours" (Max Vangeli and An21 Mix) – 8B

34. Joachim Garraud – "The Computer" (Kaskade Mix) – 8A

35. Late Night Alumni – "Finally Found" (Max Vangeli Mix) – 7A

36. David Guetta – "Paris" – 6A

37. Alex Kenji, Starkillers, and Nadia Ali – "Pressure" (Alesso Mix) – 5A

38. Sander Van Dorn – "Koko" (Bingo Players Mix) – 5A

Each of the 38 songs in this two-hour mix is mixed up or down on the Camelot Wheel one key at a time, so it's perfectly harmonic. The mix includes several of Kaskade's own mashups, which contain vocals of his tracks mixed with beats or melodies of other songs—all in the same key. The Camelot wheel does what it says it does; it simplifies harmonic mixing.

Most of the world's top DJs use the same technique. The next time you listen to your favorite DJ's live set, mixtape, or podcast, listen carefully to the transitions. If you have the tracks, run them through Mixed In Key and study the mix. Was each transition harmonically compatible?

Creating the Perfect DJ Mix

If you haven't noticed by now, we like analyzing music, and one trend we've discovered is that many successful mixes follow a certain formula. We've pored over the mixes created by hundreds of top DJs, and uncovered a sequence that they appear to rely on frequently. These are the magic ingredients that can help you create the perfect DJ mix:

1. Your first track must be an instrumental (no vocals).

2. Your second track must have vocals.

3. The duration of your first track must be shorter than 2 minutes 30 seconds.

4. The duration of your second track must be shorter than 4 minutes.

5. All subsequent tracks must be shorter than 5 minutes.

This trend appears on many successful DJ mixes. Try it yourself to see how it feels; it's not just the times that matter, but your song choices as well. Your mix may vary if your time is limited by a radio show or the rules of a contest, but this formula should provide a good foundation to help you get started.

We've had 50 thousand fans in our community read about this approach, and we've received a lot of positive feedback about it. There are a few reasons why we think it works. For one, the audience never has a chance to get bored. Second, the instrumental intro gives you the option to play a voiceover (listen to Pete Tong on BBC Radio 1 for some of the best), which does a lot to engage the crowd. Lastly, by mixing quickly, you're making a statement about your level of expertise to your audience. Anyone can play a 15-minute track and mix into another 15-minute track, but if you mix quickly, you're showcasing your talent as a DJ and showing the audience that you're in control. Once you've established your authority and that you are leading the night, you can play each track longer (up to 5 minutes).

As with everything in this book, rules are meant to be broken, so we encourage experimentation. But if you haven't tried this formula already, we urge you to give it a test drive the next time you mix.

Markus Schulz: Mixing the Perfect Set

Founder of the dance label Coldharbour Recordings, Markus Schulz has been tearing up the trance scene for years, and is always open to sharing advice with fellow DJs. When we caught up with him, we asked him how he structures the perfect club set.

When you show up at a nightclub, what elements make it enjoyable and fun to play?

MS: The first thing is that the vibe is right. What I mean by the vibe is that the opening DJ is setting up the room properly. The sound has to be great. People should be in a party mood, but the cork should not be popped just yet. When the headliner comes on, they want to make a good impression on the audience. I enjoy events where everybody on your team wants to make it a special night. The opening DJ has to be on-board, and if there's a closing DJ, they should understand how to play after the headliner. Those nights turn out to be amazing.

How should an opening DJ play?

MS: You can visualize it by looking at a graphic equalizer. The bass is on the left, and the highs are on the right. I like opening DJs who play from the center to the left part of the spectrum, focusing mostly on the beats and the bass. I want the low-end to be grooving, but I want them to avoid playing anything with a lot of hi-hats and white noise. Even if you play a slow track at 125 BPM, if it has a lot of white noise and big riffs, it fatigues people's ear drums. I like to play for ten hours and longer at a party, and if you burn people's eardrums too early, they might leave before you want them to. You want to save the high frequencies until the right time.

Should the opening DJ play music at a low volume?

MS: I don't believe that. The opening DJ can play loud. The volume isn't the issue. For me, hi-hat frequencies determine the amount of fatigue caused by the music. Even at low volume, those hi-hats can get tiresome after a while.

Is there a substantial difference between playing on the radio and playing in clubs?

MS: When I play on my radio show, I am more open to letting tracks breathe. When people are listening to the radio, you have them captivated, and you can play tracks that sound good in the headphones and have different layers. When you play in a club, you have to get to the point, and the melodies and riffs have to be more upfront.

It used to be that you could play 10-minute tracks in clubs. On the radio, you'd play the four-minute long versions. But it seems like things have reversed; now you have a more patient audience on the radio, and a shorter attention span in the clubs. I find that during a club performance, you play 4-5 minutes of each song and move on to the next one.

Playing at a festival, your performance is even more condensed. If there are five different stages and 25 different DJs, people would get bored and go to another stage if you played a song for ten minutes.

Most music productions are still 6-8 minutes long these days. Which parts do you choose to play when you have to condense the music to make it shorter?

MS: I'll play the main riff and the "big" parts of the song.

Let's talk about the "art of the opening." Let's say you have a great opening DJ who's warming up the room

and you're about to start playing in 20 minutes. What should he do at the end of his set?

MS: I recommend playing percussive music—no vocals, no big riffs. Just start getting more percussive. You're setting a groove. People are starting to find their spots for the headlining DJ to come on.

Sometimes it happens that the opening DJ will do a great job, but then he starts playing anthems right before the headliner to get the crowd hyped up. This is actually not what you want to do. When the headlining DJ comes on, and the cork is popped, it's supposed to be a big dramatic entrance for them. To set that up, try to build anticipation with good grooves.

But I have to tell you something. Out of hundreds of thousands of DJs out there, the smallest percentage know how to properly open up for a headliner. As a headlining DJ, when we find someone who does it RIGHT, we request them every time. I think some people don't realize how many headlining DJs are always looking for the ultimate opening DJ. If we find one, we hang onto them. We even take them on the road with us.

It's interesting that there is a "closing DJ" as well—the person who plays after the headliner leaves. What is their job exactly?

MS: I think they have a difficult job. If the headliner is famous, people may want to leave after they get off. My advice for the closing DJ is to play a lot of classics. I always say, start with a classic track after the headliner has left. Journey to a genre where the headliner didn't go.

When I play my longer sets, I program my music as three different DJs in my head. In my opening set, I play progressive. In my peak-hour set, I play the typical Markus Schulz set. In the after-hours, I play more twisted music mixed with classics. If you play safe and commercial after the headliner, you're not going to stand out. But people will stay if there's something special and significant that they haven't heard that same night already.

How would you transition from a headliner set to a closing set?

MS: I would mix out of the headlining DJ's track if he allows you to, and mix into your own music to get into a more groovy vibe. The problem is, an abrupt change in tempo could lose the energy of the crowd, so a continuous mix is actually better for the club and you.

You travel constantly for your gigs, and it's quite different from playing in your home town. What do you usually carry with you when you travel?

MS: You have to get used to packing light. I do not check in any luggage, so everything I take on the road with me is carry-on only. It's simple: take some pants for travel, two or three for the shows and get your clothes laundered at the hotel during the tour. Every hotel has laundry service. You shouldn't check your luggage if you travel a lot. It will always get lost somewhere, and you won't get it back until the end of your tour because it will always be one or two days behind you.

I also suggest keeping your DJ set foolproof. You should be flexible—you don't always know what gear the club will have, and you should be able to roll with whatever happens. Play on the gear, and move onto the next show without getting frustrated over the technicalities. Obviously, your contract rider should spell out what you need, but keep your needs as simple as possible so there is less room for error.

One thing I always say is that it's easy to prepare for a few weeks, drive down to your local club, and throw down an amazing set. But traveling, showing up jet-lagged and not knowing if it's day or night, and playing an amazing set for people who paid to see you is a lot more challenging. It's always nice to not worry about the gear. You're there to make the party happen, and you can do it easier if your DJ equipment requirements are simple.

I am sure you carry around backups of your music too.

MS: Right. I'm playing from a hard drive now, and I make sure that all CDJs are linked together. I also carry some SD cards that have at least the last month of music backed up on them. One time when I was in Turkey, I got to the gig and when I was just about to start, I realized that I left the main USB stick in my hotel room. I only had a backup with me. I had to play, but I sent someone to my hotel room. For the first 30 minutes, I played off my backup until they came back with my main music collection. I couldn't imagine if I didn't have a backup what would have happened.

It would have been an oldies night...

MS: I didn't even have that. Always have a backup. The show must go on!

We've seen your Winter Music Conference panels in Miami where you've shared advice with people. During your career, you've always helped DJs learn more about what you know. Since social media is such an important part of marketing for DJs lately, what's your approach?

MS: I think that with social media, fans want to know who you are when you're not on the decks. If they really love your music and your sets, they want to know more about you. Social media helps you stay connected with fans on a more personal level. I notice that different types of posts generate different kinds of feedback. You could produce a new track and say "Hey, this is my new track," but when you put up a more personal item like "I'm working here in the studio, here's a photo," it seems to connect better with fans because they can see the process. When you post a picture of yourself in a studio, it gives your fans a look at what it was like. I think the theatre of the mind is still a very powerful thing.

What is a good way to get local gigs?

MS: The biggest thing is experience. I started by playing at the smallest clubs inside hotels. It helped me read the crowd and set up the mood for the night. I think young DJs need to find some gigs and residencies at small places just to start establishing a feeling for what it's like to DJ from beginning to end.

There are two types of DJs. One is the guy who had a hit record and goes on tour as a result. Most of the time these guys will play one or two-hour sets, and that's it. They have to learn how to DJ in order to perform because they have a hit record.

The other type is a DJ who came up from the art of DJing. That's one of the biggest things I want people to understand, that there is an *art* to DJing. As this music blows up and becomes even more mainstream, learning the art of DJing through small residencies and small clubs will put you further ahead when you break. When you finally make it, you will have more experience, and it will come through in your DJ sets if you learn the art now.

What about a situation where a DJ lives in a city that doesn't have a strong community supporting his favorite music genre? For example, let's say that someone lives in Kansas City. Does it make sense to play commercial music just for experience?

MS: Well, it doesn't have to be a club. It can be a coffee shop or a restaurant. You can play anywhere to learn how to set the mood.

What if you don't want to sell out and play too commercial?

MS: It's true that a restaurant may not want to hear Swedish House Mafia or my tracks during dinner, but you can still find a way to DJ. It's absolutely possible. When I started, I was playing in places that wanted Top 40 music. My passion was for more underground music, but I learned how to program and how to read the crowds in those Top 40 places. When I started playing underground places, that knowledge was invaluable.

I remember the club would close at 2 o'clock. I would go home, power on my turntables and spin for another two hours for myself, like I was playing at an afterparty. That way, when I was invited to play afterparties, I was already in the groove because I've learned how to do it at home. When I first started, I would stumble after half an hour or 45 minutes. The next night, I'd go to the club, come home and do the same thing. Eventually, I mastered the sound I was trying to achieve. It helped me learn and it made a huge difference.

11. Learn How to DJ in Nightclubs

Nightclubs have always played a key role in supporting and promoting DJ culture. Without venues like The Sanctuary, The Loft and Studio 54, the *business* of modern DJing might not be the diversified and unstoppable force that it is today. It's now routine for festival organizers, club owners, talent buyers and promoters to book huge events and entire tours around superstar DJs like David Guetta, Tiësto, deadmau5, Paul van Dyk and many more.

Modern DJing has evolved into an international business, but nightclubs are still a vital proving ground for established DJs, as well as the up-and-comers. A good DJ is always prepared to play different styles on different occasions. Whether you're opening the night to an empty dance floor or headlining a packed club, each occasion has its own demands—and this extends to recording mixtapes, entering mix competitions, or spinning live radio sets too. Every set you do is a statement about who you are as a DJ, so it's important to be diligent in all your preparations, especially when you're dealing with booking agents, talent buyers and club managers.

Your First Gig: Managing Expectations

You have to learn how to work with a variety of people to have a successful DJ career. If you're playing a club gig, your point of contact is usually the general manager. Club owners can be hands-off, or they may own multiple properties and won't be in the building every time you play.

Is the owner experienced or new to nightlife? If you're working for an inexperienced club owner, he or she might be unaccustomed to paying DJs well, or might have unrealistic expectations and be prone to making rash decisions. Experienced owners can offer more stability, with a deeper understanding of the nightlife industry and a more professional staff—all of which makes your job easier—but they might also have a formula for success that conflicts with your own. Either way, if you can help an owner make a lot of money, this will lead to more opportunities—among them, curating your own night at the club.

But first things first: Talk to the general manager before your gig, and set expectations before you walk in the door. You need to know what types of music you will be expected to play, and what to avoid (and whether, for example, there are any required or prohibited songs). You also need to understand the flow of a typical night: When does the club get crowded? What is an average night of bar sales? What does the owner consider a successful night?

Nightclubs often take on the personality of their owners, so your experience will vary. Pay attention to the way the owners advertise, the way they've designed the club, and their vision for success. And if you secure a residency, get to know the club's regulars. If you see the same people every week, it's wise to switch up your DJ set so that you sound fresh every time.

It's always smart to arrive early on gig night, especially if you haven't played the venue previously. Get to know the bartenders, table hosts, and doormen, and be polite and professional—they may help you get booked again. Most importantly, get to know the customers. They may be there to see you, but the night is really for them, and they spend the money that keeps the club in business.

How to Approach an Opening Set

Opening for another DJ can often be more challenging than headlining. An effective opening set can be the determining factor in whether a club night is successful, yet many club owners and promoters seem to overlook the importance of an opening DJ's role.

In most cases, a headliner never plays the entire night. Many events feature one or more DJs opening up for the headlining act. As the opening DJ, you need to be aware of the progression of the night and always show restraint. The key is to build up the energy gradually so you can set up a smooth transition to the headliner's set.

This is why playing a proper warm-up set can be one of the most difficult tasks for a DJ. You have to push your ego to the side, and focus on playing a balanced set that creates the right mood for the headliner. Many young DJs make the mistake of playing tracks with too much energy, or they throw caution to the wind and start playing all the hits. This almost always disrupts the flow of the night, and ends up confusing the crowd, upsetting management, and frustrating the headliner. Your career will be a short one if you approach an opening set this way.

Most of the time, you have to start with an empty room that slowly fills with people—and they're usually sober. Pay close attention to how they react to what you play, and how each track in your set affects the mood of the room. This is your opportunity to play music you love and to learn to read a crowd. It's best to think of it as a challenge; if it's an hour before midnight and you can pull a group of sober people onto the dance floor, you'll probably have no problem getting a group of drunken revelers to dance at 1:30 in the morning.

Always research the headliner so you can tailor your set according to his or her style. If you're opening for

Kaskade, for example, you wouldn't play the same tracks as you would opening for Skrillex. (And remember, you should *never* play any tracks produced by the headliner during your set.) The challenge is to get different crowds dancing while complementing the main act at the same time.

Regardless of whether there are three or 300 people on the dance floor, you're getting paid for a specific job. The club depends on you to create an atmosphere, keep the crowd entertained as the alcohol begins to flow, and fill up the dance floor slowly so that it's full when the headliner begins. If you're playing bangers at 11 o'clock for an empty dance floor, the headliner has nowhere to go but down. You may think you're showcasing your skills to a club owner, but you're really just showing your inexperience. Prove yourself as a strong opening DJ, and you'll get booked again—maybe next time as a headliner.

In the end, it's wise to look at the opening set as a vehicle for developing your personal style as an artist. Successful club owners and event organizers have always recognized that a reliable opening DJ is vital for preparing the foundation of a great show.[18] If you make it clear that

---

[18] Jack O'Shaughnessy. "The Esoteric Art of the Opening DJ," September 22, 2009. http://www.residentadvisor.net/feature.aspx?1095.

you're a music lover who's prepared to play for any
audience, you'll be in demand for more gigs.

The Art of Headlining

Once you've mastered the opening set, you're ready to
headline your own night. As the headlining DJ, you'll be
responsible for playing the hottest songs during peak time
at the club. You'll have to learn how to read the crowd so
you can adapt accordingly. Are people dancing and having
fun? Are they buying drinks? If you're keeping the bar
busy, you're keeping the club owner happy.

You can't be a headliner if you don't have a stage
presence. The crowd feeds off your energy, so if you look
bored, you'll lose them. When laptop DJing started going
mainstream in the mid-2000s, the joke among disgruntled
fans was often "The DJ is checking his email!" Always
make eye contact with your audience and take in what's in
front of you on the dance floor instead of staring at your
laptop all night. DJing is all about interacting with the
crowd—not hiding behind a laptop screen.

To prepare for your headline gig, do your research on
the club first, and then set up a meeting with the club
owner, manager, or promoter to discuss what's expected.
Listen to the music DJs play there, and keep tabs on the
crowd's reaction. It's also smart to talk with the bar staff

and find out the general mood and tastes of the people who frequent the club. Information is power; if you prepare for your set with this in mind, you can avoid surprises later and focus on connecting with your audience.

Club Lighting

A well-designed lighting system has a huge impact on a venue. The biggest festivals and best shows often coordinate changes in lighting patterns with the DJ's music.

Premier club venues have lighting operators who can customize the atmosphere to reflect the music of the moment. But many beginning DJs don't have the opportunity to play regularly in venues with lighting engineers. As you get started, familiarize yourself with the lighting console available at your venue. Experiment with the lighting effects before the club gets crowded, and pre-set some lighting routines if you can.

Varying the light system's groupings and intensity can add ambiance, set the mood, and boost the energy. Lighting is not just about repetitive strobe effects. Intelligent lighting instruments can pan, tilt, focus, dim, color, and shape beams. Specific colors can even influence mental states; red is a warm color, blue is cool, and green is calm. Part of a venue's success rides on how well you can integrate these lighting elements with the music to create a coordinated experience on the dance floor, so if you're working with a lighting operator, make sure to meet beforehand to work out some routines.

Biz Martinez: The Business of DJ Bookings

As the music director and talent buyer at one of the hottest clubs in Miami, Biz Martinez has become an influential presence on the dance music scene. We asked him about his booking strategy, and what he looks for in up-and-coming DJs.

Every week, the DJ lineup at LIV Miami is one of the best in the country. How do you coordinate your DJ schedule?

Biz: Each night has an identity or a sound. We start by programming to fit the identity of the target audience for each night, so the nights contrast with each other as much as possible.

Tell us about the DJ booking process. What are you looking for?

Biz: Besides the obvious industry giants, I usually look for fresh and of-the-moment talent that we can introduce and help grow. This involves knowing who's about to surface in the dance world and/or pop culture. The booking process is simple: the two fundamental intro steps are finding out who represents the artist, and when the artist will be available. Being the first club to make a formal offer on a future star is key.

A-list DJs aren't easy to get in competitive markets like Miami, New York, and Vegas. A great venue and deep pockets are just as important as having a solid relationship with the talent agents and management.

Some of the booking fees for artists who play at LIV exceed $20,000 a night. From a business standpoint, how can LIV afford so much for a great DJ? Does table service really earn that much money?

Biz: If you're looking to book talent near or above $20K in Miami, volume is everything. Table service allows us to take in big profits, ensuring us a return on our investment. Our club and organization are designed for high volume based on per-head spending.

You have several resident DJs who play every week. How did they get the gig?

Biz: Some resident DJs like Ross One have been with us since year one. He's our most versatile DJ and usually plays our indie dance/hip-hop nights. Mednas is our go-to house music guy. He has an understanding and knowledge of how to warm up a room and play alongside the big names. Both these guys are talented enough to headline their own nights, but they also know the importance of playing their roles alongside special guests. On top of that, they're human music encyclopedias in their respective genres.

What are the key factors an up-and-coming DJ should focus on to get booked?

Biz: Get out, network, and see and hear what's hot—but also get in the studio and make music. Guys like Calvin Harris and Avicii have acquired large followings because they produce big records and play a lot of their own music, from remixes to originals to edits. That's what makes them special, and that's what gets them gigs. Eat, sleep, and breathe music.

What's your advice for someone who is new to Miami and wants to get established as a local DJ?

Biz: Again, get out and network. Get your music in the right hands and get noticed. Promote and market yourself or find someone to help you. Once you land the gig, make sure you deliver and build from there. Be patient, learn how to take criticism, gather experience, and evolve. Chances are, as incredible as your mom says you are, you ain't no genius.

Do you ever get a phone call from a top DJ's agent saying, "We'll be in Miami in three months. Do you have a gig available?" Is that common practice?

Biz: Sure, but it *only* happens after you've established yourself as a player in your market, built a relationship, and earned their trust. It's an agent's job to make the artist money and make the artist desirable, but also to ensure the artist is in good hands.

LIV has a successful hip-hop night on Sundays. Do the same rules of DJing apply to hip-hop and house?

Biz: I gotta give it to the hip-hop guys. Those dudes drop three times the amount of records most house guys drop. While house guys seamlessly weave their way through tracks, hip-hop guys slice records in and out every 45 to 90 seconds. Much respect!

Understanding Nightlife

Nightlife is big business. A 2004 report from Audience Research & Analysis calculated that the nightlife industry in New York City alone generated an estimated $9.7 billion in economic activity, $2.6 billion in earnings (primarily wages), and 95,500 jobs on a yearly basis.[19] The same study found that annual attendance at NYC nightlife venues totaled an estimated 65,445,000 admissions, which was

---

[19] Audience Research & Analysis. "The $9 Billion Economic Impact of the Nightlife Industry on New York City: A Study of Spending by Bar/Lounges and Clubs/Music Venues and Their Attendees," January 2004.
http://www.nysra.org/associations/2487/files/EconomicStudy.pdf.

"more than three times the attendance of all New York City's sports teams combined."[20]

No matter how talented or technically adept you might be, if you're going to embark on a career as a DJ, you need to understand how the nightlife industry really works. It may look like a constant party on the surface, but a club is in business to *make money*. Employees at the best nightclubs are sociable, smart professionals who often don't drink on the job. This is a hospitality industry, and the music, atmosphere, aesthetics and staff are all meant to help the bottom line.

If you want a career in nightlife, it's smart to become familiar with how a club operates. You can shadow different staff members on your night off or before your set. Does the club have a strict door policy? Watch the doorman work for a night. What kind of vibe is he trying to create with the clientele? To understand how the table and bottle service works, you can follow a VIP host for a night. Many clubs generate a significant portion of their revenue from bottle service clients, who may be celebrities, professionals, bankers or socialites. Part of your job as a DJ is to help the venue keep these valued clients happy.

---

[20] Ibid.

Customers pay to let loose at a club and escape the stress of their daily lives. They might be there to hear the music, to enjoy the feeling of exclusivity, to meet new people, or to have fun with friends, but they chose your venue. Your job as a DJ is to make sure they have fun, spend money, and come back again for more.

Music is a must in any hospitality setting. Studies show that the right combination of music at any venue where guests have come to relax and enjoy themselves contributes to overall customer satisfaction, and to the likelihood that they'll return.[21] Whether it's a busy bar or restaurant, a laid-back lounge, or a high-energy club, music programming engages the guests to stay and spend.

Do certain music styles increase spending? What about playing certain songs at certain points of the night? The more you understand about the club and its guests, the better your set will be, and the more likely you'll be invited back.

Also keep in mind that studies have tied popular music to economic conditions. Researchers have proven a direct correlation between the Dow Jones Industrial Average and

---

[21] Michael Harrelson. "Not Just Background Music," *Night Club and Bar Magazine*, April 17, 2009. http://www.nightclub.com/music-entertainment/not-just-background-music.

the key and tempo of popular songs[22]. In 2008, after the stock market crashed, club-goers wanted to faster-paced, minor-key electronic music. Economic busts are associated with up-tempo, sad-sounding music in minor keys, while economic booms are linked to down-tempo, happy-sounding songs in major keys.

"The data has been consistent from the 1960s to today," says Yale Fox, editor of the blog Darwin vs. the Machine (www.darwinvsthemachine.com). "There is a correlation between stock market performance and the tempo and key of music popular on the *Billboard* charts. Along with vocals, tempo and key are two of the most emotional elements of music."

According to Fox, there's a reason why house music is more popular in a down economy. "House was underground forever," he says. "When the economy is hurting, music labels are hurting like everybody else. A lot of electronic music can be produced at home without being in a fancy studio, so it levels the playing field. More underground music genres, like electronic, tend to come out when the economy dips."

---

[22] "TEDxIB @ York – Yale Fox – Nightclubs As Research Labs," YouTube video uploaded by TEDxTalks, January 23, 2012. http://www.youtube.com/watch?v=MSShNSgOAR0.

"House music is up-tempo and has more energy," Fox continues. "We live in an instant gratification generation. The peaks and valleys that build and release in house music tease the crowd and make people feel good. If you go to a Swedish House Mafia show, the room is going to look a certain way. You'll see a lot of hands in the air. You'll see a lot of women in the crowd."

Strategic Group owners Jason Strauss and Noah Tepperberg have built an empire of successful venues—including TAO, Lavo, and Marquee—by focusing on building relationships with customers[23]. As a DJ, if there's one lesson to be learned from two of the best nightlife operators in the country, it's that the music you play contributes to the atmosphere as well as the bottom line. Studio 54 co-owner and legendary hotel designer Ian Schrager has put it best. "When you're in the nightclub business, you have no discernible product," he says. "You have nothing different from everybody else. Same liquor, same music. The only opportunity for distinction is the magic you create."[24]

---

[23] Anita Elberse, Ryan Barlow, and Sheldon Wong. "Marquee: The Business of Nightlife," February 25, 2009.
http://noahtepperberg.com/wp-content/uploads/Harvard-Business-School-Case-Study.pdf.

[24] Sara Stosic. "Marketing the Illusion of Inclusive Exclusivity," (New York University, 2011). Accessed January 30, 2012.

12. Build Your Brand

Your marketable skills begin with your talent and your sound, but there's more to this picture too—your consistency, dedication, professionalism and personality carry a lot of weight with your fans *and* with the people who want to hire you.

At the "superstar" level, DJs are a unique breed because they have to manage multiple aspects of their public persona. It's not enough just to tour the world with an expensive light show, or to mix a mind-blowing set with passion and creativity. You literally have to be an arbiter of *the future*—attuned to emerging trends and technologies, and ahead of the curve with your selections, remixes, and productions—while *still* maintaining a vestige of the sound and style that got you there. That's not easy; just ask Tiësto, BT and Richie Hawtin, or even eclectic outliers like Ellen Allien or Amon Tobin, both of whom have reinvented themselves more times than we can count, but draw packed houses consistently.

---

http://guerrillaculinary.files.wordpress.com/2012/01/marketing-the-illusion-of-inclusive-exclusivity.pdf.

If you're just starting out as a DJ, we know it feels great to drop a mix that really shakes up your local club. But if you're looking to pursue this as a career, where do you go from here? Defining and curating your brand is really the key to moving forward.

Why Does Branding Matter for DJs?

Think about the most successful DJs in the world, and you'll realize that they have several things in common besides their technical skills and talent. They each have a distinctive sound, look and personality, and they each maintain a steady media presence—all of which connects to being memorable as a brand. Tiësto is a perfect example; with his immediately recognizable logo and his dynamic presence on stage or in the booth (he's known for dancing all night), his live shows have become ritual gatherings for his fans worldwide.

Elements like these are important in furthering your own DJ career. You need to create your own identity so you can stand out from the crowd of DJs who are available to play on any given night in any given city. Competition for residencies is always fierce, so you'll need an edge to get ahead.

Think again about your favorite DJs. You know what to expect each time you hear Kaskade, Tiësto, Avicii, or Skrillex play a set. They have built their brand around a specific sound and image. This isn't to say that they're playing it *safe*—after all, if your fanbase learns to expect you to change with every album, that too can become part of your brand—but consistency is at the core of what they do every night, whether they're on tour or in the studio.

Creating and Curating Your Image

The way you dress and the music you play, as well as your social media presence, website, and the marketing materials you create, are all reflections of your personal brand. But don't forget why you need it: you're trying to get gigs so you can make a living playing music. If you're not getting work, or if you feel stuck in a creative rut, you might want to think about retooling your brand.

Back in 2010, New York City DJ Danny Rockz made a name for himself in a flooded market by reinventing his image. After a decade of DJing on the local scene, Rockz had begun to lose interest and decided to start over with a clean slate. "I took the first two months of 2010 to think about what I wanted to do, what direction I wanted to head in," he says. "I started with a whole new image and a new music format. I started doing parties I liked and playing music I liked, and it all just grew from there."[25]

Rockz adopted a true open-format mix in his live sets to include rock and roll, indie, house, hip-hop and classics from every era. Eventually, he landed a residency at Provocateur and regular gigs at such New York hot spots as 1OAK, The Darby and Gansevoort Park. "You have to make yourself stand out in some way," he observes. "Personality is the one thing I feel like a lot of people lack."[26]

Not only do you need to decide which market you want to target (whether private events, bars and lounges, or the full-on bottle service scene at local clubs), but you need to cultivate an ability to network. "I talk to people, meet people and follow through," Rockz says. "A lot of times you have to stay on top of people, but in the sense that you're not overwhelming or creepy about it. You just want to be cool—just say, 'Hey, what's going on? How are we going to make this happen?'"[27]

---

[25] Bonnie Gleicher. "DJ Danny Rockz on Life As a Professional Party Starter," *BlackBook*, January 19, 2012.
http://www.blackbookmag.com/nightlife/dj-danny-rockz-on-life-as-a-professional-party-starter-1.44076.

[26] Ibid.

[27] Ibid.

Interview with Ani Quinn: DJing in the Big City of Dreams

As one of the top DJs in New York City, Ani Quinn has made the most out of his early experiences on the city's underground rave scene. We asked him what the competition is like in one of the toughest markets in the world.

How did you become a resident at your current clubs?

AQ: It helps if you're an exceptional DJ. I've worked hard over the years to hone my skills. But all of the current residencies I have are based on my relationships with club owners and promoters. Some of these relationships I've had since grammar school. But these guys didn't hire me to

DJ just because they know me. I can hold a room, and I consistently throw down a solid set. But it really is true what they say: it's all about who you know.

Is New York City nightlife different from other parts of the world?

AQ: Hip-hop is still huge in NYC. On any given night at clubs like 1OAK, Greenhouse, SL or Avenue, you might have Jay-Z, Busta Rhymes, or Russell Simmons in the building listening to your set. Obviously, if Jay-Z is in the club with Kanye West, you're going to play more of their music than you would otherwise. It depends on the venue, though. A lot of spots want more of an open format set and don't want DJs to play too much urban music.

Overall, New York has a huge and diverse nightlife scene. You've got clubs that cater strictly to EDM, and you've got spots that just want indie music. There are different clubs for different crowds, and different nights at different spots, to cater to people's needs. On the weekends, clubs tend to loosen up their door policy. There are more tourists and "bridge and tunnel" crowds from Jersey out in the city. DJs tend to play more commercial sets to cater to the weekend crowds.

If I play outside of New York, I try to make sure I know what the crowd wants for that specific venue. People book me knowing that I'm a New York DJ, so they expect me to bring that flavor to my sets. But different cities and clubs have different sounds. Ultimately, I want the crowd to enjoy themselves, so I try to find out beforehand what works for the specific night that I'm DJing. I'm not going to hold a club hostage and force the audience to listen to one thing when it really wants another.

Everyone does it differently, but how do you read the crowd and decide what to play? Are there any "tells" that help you figure out what to do next?

AQ: I just keep my eye on the room. A good DJ can tell when it's time to switch up the vibe. It's really about movement. If the room isn't moving, then I need to switch it up. In actuality, there are so many different ways to DJ. Most parties these days want non-stop high energy from beginning to end, with no ebb or flow in the music. If it's just about keeping the energy up, I know which records to play and when, and I'm not opposed to playing some of the bigger songs multiple times in one night. If the crowd is a little cooler, I might test out records to see their response or play stuff that I just want to hear and that I think sounds good with my current song selection. But I always have a group of songs ready that I know will bring the energy back up in the room. It's also about being confident in your song selection and your ability to put it all together. It's great when you're able to play something that the crowd doesn't expect but you've timed it in a way that still works for the room.

Tell us how your residency works. You come to the club before it opens, and what happens next? What's a typical night in terms of the time you spend in the venue?

AQ: I used to get to the club early and get set up before the doors were open, but now I have openers and closers. I typically hit them up to see how the night is looking so I know what to expect when I get there. I usually arrive around 12:30 a.m. and then go on right at peak time. I immediately try to bring the energy up a few notches. I have a bunch of great openers that I use. They know not to play certain records, but I'm not opposed to them running a few of the bigger tracks. I know I can go on and still kill the party, even if the DJ spinning before me really has the crowd rocking.

Do you get to know the general manager and the promoters? How much input do they have on the music?

AQ: It's important to have relationships with the staff in nightclubs. If you work somewhere every week for years at a time, it's inevitable that you'll get to know your co-workers. Everyone is on the same team, from the owners and promoters to the waitresses and bartenders to the busboys and bathroom attendants. Successful weekly nights have a life of their own. The music is a huge factor, but if the doorman isn't doing a good job, the night's not going to go as smoothly. If security isn't on point, all sorts of problems can arise. I have the utmost respect for any nightclub staff, whether I've worked with them for 10 years or for only one night.

We talk about the financial side of the business in this book. Do any of the clubs put you on salary, or are you always paid per gig?

AQ: It's a pay-per-gig situation. I've been offered salaries from nightclubs before, but I make better money working different spots. It's also important to keep things new and fresh. While good weekly parties are priceless and help build a DJ's reputation and career, if you get stuck working at one venue, it can limit your exposure to new listeners and new opportunities. No club or night stays hot forever, and as a DJ, you have to stay one step ahead of that curve. If a long residency starts to lose steam, sometimes it's better to move on to something new even if it means a little downtime between parties.

Do you ever get to choose your opening DJs?

AQ: I use my own openers and closers as much as possible. It's how I started DJing. It's how I got my foot in the door, and I try to do the same thing for new DJs. A lot of the openers I've used have gone on to DJ their own nights. I think it's awesome that I could help give someone that kind of opportunity.

Four Marketing Tools You Absolutely Need

You have to start somewhere. In Chapter 13, we'll get into more detail about social media and how you can use online marketing to your advantage. For now though, here are four essential tools you need to start marketing yourself to the world.

1. **Logo**: An eye-catching and unique logo shows that you've invested time and creativity in your brand. The most successful DJs in the world have customized logos. We'll show you a few ways you can create one.

2. **Promotional Photos**: Your personality and how you present yourself as an artist are vital for landing new gigs. Most venues will happily put your image on a flyer, which from there usually gets posted on Facebook, the venue's website and printed materials. It's built-in advertising for you and your brand.

3. **Business Cards**: A smart, professional-looking business card speaks volumes about you; it's often your first point of entry with promoters, club owners or anyone else, including fans, who can get you gigs. It's better than just trading phone numbers.

A well-designed card makes an impression that people will remember when you call them to follow up.

4. **Facebook Page**: This is not your personal Facebook Profile, which is where you can add friends. A Page allows you to build your fanbase and post news about upcoming events, new mixes and remixes, video clips and even merchandise. It also improves your chances of showing up near the top of a Google search (known as search engine optimization, or SEO). We talk a bit more about Facebook in Chapter 13.

Design Your Logo

You don't necessarily need a flair for graphic design to create an effective logo—just a little patience and a willingness to experiment. Most DJs don't have a logo, so if you can come up with a unique symbol or a customized font to promote your name, you're already a step ahead of the competition.

Getting started. Spend some time thinking about your DJ name and your image. Try to come up with five to ten variations of your name and some symbols that inspire you, and then sketch them on paper. Your symbol should fit your music, so think about the music you play most often and what associations you can take from that. If you play friendly and vocal house music, then you might consider going with an elegant and smooth font, or a design with clean lines. If you favor minimal and techy music, you might be better suited to a font and logo with sharp edges and prominent corners.

Take a quick look at the websites of a few well-known DJs, and you'll see that most logos are horizontal and will easily fit in a rectangular box. This size and shape is also easy to fit on business cards, promotional materials, and custom websites. For example, take a look at Kaskade's old logo:

Before changing his style, Kaskade played soulful house music with great melodies. The leaves and vines that wind around the letters of his name are a good sign that you won't get banging drum-and-bass when you listen to his music. Small details like this can make a good logo even better.

Try a few different designs. It's a good idea to come up with a few options that you like, and then ask your friends for their honest opinion—they can be a great resource for input and ideas. Once you have a design and color scheme that you're happy with, draw a large, clean version of it. This is your chance to get creative; you can add details, play with the color, or think about embellishments. Try experimenting with new fonts to see if anything strikes you.

When you create the final sketch, you'll have to convert it to an Adobe Illustrator file and a transparent .PNG file that you can use on various websites. You can hire a graphic designer to help you with this, or ask your friends and see who might have the software you need. In our experience, it's easy to find a graphic designer among your friends.

Sometimes a simple font is just as good as a logo. If you don't have access to a designer, you can just choose a font to represent your name. You don't need a symbol or a complex idea; good typography can be just as memorable. There are plenty of font sellers online (such as Fonts.com) that allow you to preview different fonts before you buy them. All you need to do is type your name into the preview window, and you'll see how it looks in the font that you've chosen.

Fortunately, there are legitimate websites where you can get fonts for free too. If the website has a good reputation and respects copyright, you're not violating copyright for using those fonts. DaFont.com is one of them. We typed in the name *Beyond Beatmatching* and got a large list of results, many of which we thought would be perfect for a DJ logo.

Don't be afraid to make changes. Even though you've done a lot of work so far, your logo is not necessarily set in stone. Everything goes through an evolutionary process, and you might have better ideas two years from now. The important thing is that you take action now—the sooner, the better.

For inspiration, take a look at a flyer below and study the DJ logos. This came from the 2011 Ultra Music Festival; it's a great example of how a logo's look and shape affects readability. Each one has a unique font, is easily read at a glance, and fits snugly into the rectangular format we mentioned above.

Take Promotional Photos

Before you don your headphones and run out looking for a graffiti-covered wall or a crowded club where you can do your Christ pose for the camera, think about some of your favorite DJ flyers. Most of the major headlining DJs portray a provocative and sophisticated look, but they're not afraid to invoke a little humor when the occasion calls for it. Here's a flyer promoting Kaskade at the Marquee Las Vegas. What image do you think it conveys?

Keep in mind that your DJ photos will be printed on flyers, so the edges need to blend to black or white easily. Waist-up or headshot photos are often the best, and unless you can afford a new photo shoot every six months, try to go for a timeless look.

Check out the following pictures of David Guetta. One was taken earlier in his career, and the other was taken in 2011, the year he was voted No. 1 in the *DJ Mag* Top 100 poll. Which one looks more current and professional?

Choose the right camera. You need to put some thought into how you take your pictures. There's some useful research online that can help you with this. Dating website OKCupid has sampled 552,000 user photos and aggregated 11.4 million opinions about them, with some very interesting results.[28]

Two factors that play a major role in photo quality are the shutter speed and lens. Even the type and brand of camera you use will have a huge effect on how good you look. Interchangeable lens cameras (like digital SLRs) make you look more attractive than your basic point-and-shoot cameras, which in turn will make you look better than the camera on your phone.

In addition, "soft light can hide wrinkles, blemishes, [and] devil eyes. The hard light of a flash often brings them out. For example, a 28 year-old who used a flash is as attractive as a 35 year-old who didn't." A direct flash often produces harsh shadows, so use a flash that can bounce off the ceiling or walls if you can. The best pictures also have a very shallow depth of field, meaning that the subject is in crisp focus while the background is blurry.

---

[28] Christian Rudder. "Don't Be Ugly by Accident!" OKCupid, August 10, 2010. http://blog.okcupid.com/index.php/dont-be-ugly-by-accident.

"Basically, you get a sharp/blurry effect from having [a] wide-open aperture (low f numbers on your camera, like $f/1.8, f/2.2$, etc.). Of two pictures taken at the same distance, the photo taken at the lower f number will feel more intimate and personal."[29]

Find the right time to take your picture. Broadly speaking, late afternoon and late night are optimal if you do your photo shoot outside. Photos taken late at night tend to be more provocative, and those taken in the early afternoon tend to be pleasantly lit. "When you overlay the path of the sun through the sky during our theoretical 'day,' [the best times] are just after sunrise and just before

---

[29] Ibid.

sunset," which is what the study refers to as the "golden hour" for taking photos.[30]

Example of a "golden light" photograph:

---

[30] Ibid.

Example of a white wall shoot:

So if you shoot outside, shoot at the golden hour. If you shoot inside, use a white or black background. And don't wear anything that would embarrass your mother.

Design Your DJ Business Card

Having a logo isn't enough to establish your brand. Despite the huge popularity of social networking platforms like Facebook and Twitter, business cards are still one of the best ways to get your name and contact information in front of the people you need to impress. A business card is a tangible reminder of you, and an easy point of reference for anyone who's interested in contacting you.

7Any random sample of 100 business cards will probably turn up just two or three that have a memorable and compelling design. We can't offer a foolproof method for creating a card that will guarantee you're among those rare few, but we have some ideas that can get you started.

Get a feel for what's out there. If you keep stacks of business cards from the people you've met over the years, flip through them and take note of which ones stand out. What drew your eye to it, and why does it make other cards look knocked-off or unprofessional? You can find plenty of other examples online; take an hour to browse the web to find cards that might work for you, and think about the elements—logo, font, design, elegance and simplicity—that make the card stand out.

The best designs are clean and easy to read. An artsy background surface can make your business card memorable, but it shouldn't interfere with its legibility. Your business card is meant to give people your name and contact information so they can get in touch with you, and that's it. You don't need to muddy it up with excessive design or decoration, so use a font that's easy to read. Use your logo if you have one, and feel free to write "Ask Me to DJ" next to your phone number and e-mail contact. If you give people a call to action, they're more likely to respond.

Don't sacrifice quality. Imagine you're walking through Miami Beach and run into the owner of the biggest club in the city. Would you give him a card that cost two cents to print? For elite business cards, choose a heavy, 100-to-120-pound paper stock and bright, high-quality ink. A rough or silk surface feels great to the touch. The best cards can cost as much as two dollars each—pretty expensive, but a huge gig will pay for a thousand cards. It's a worthy investment in your career.

There are two sides to every story. Never leave the back of your card blank. If you leave this space open, people will use it as scrap paper, and might leave the club with a phone number written on the back that isn't yours. One option is to print a dark background on the back, or you can go with a large version of your logo, or something else altogether (in Japan, for instance, most businesses print Japanese on one side and English on the other). Fans will keep your card longer if they admire what you've created.

If you don't feel comfortable creating a design for a logo or a card, work with a graphic designer to make sure you get the look you want. You're creating something that can ultimately define your career, so have fun with it.

Try this website. We love Moo.com and their templates for business cards. They have designs you can customize and print without having to learn Adobe Photoshop. Their templates will help you create a cool design in a few minutes; you can customize your name and contact information, and choose from a number of great designs to match your personality. If you don't have access to a graphic designer, we think this is the best way to create business cards yourself.

In our case, our Mixed In Key cards took about a week to ship, and the results were stunning.

Create a Press Kit

Once you've got some experience under your belt, you might find that you need to assemble a press kit. This is an informational package that provides club owners, booking agents, publicists and journalists with the materials they need to promote or write about you.

The most effective press kits are simple and elegant; if you're sending one by email (usually referred to as an electronic press kit, or EPK), you should condense it into one PDF with clickable links to your demo mixes (see below).

A typical press kit contains the following materials:

- A short, one-page **bio** that also lists the genres you play, current gigs and any residencies

- A list of **career highlights** (including press mentions, festivals you've played and DJ contests you've won)

- A high-quality **promotional photo**, or full portfolio if you have one

- Three or four **demo mixes** (These demonstrate your strengths as a DJ; focus on what you're currently playing, and organize the demos by genre.)

- Your **resume** and **contact information** (This speaks for itself; you need a current DJ resume with the names of other DJs you've worked with, as well as venues and references. If you're just starting out, skip the resume but always include your contact information.)

- Sample **flyers** (only if you've done some high-profile gigs, or if you feel one or two flyers look slick enough to include)

- Three to five **business cards** (if you're sending a physical press kit via snail mail)

When you assemble your press kit, think about what your marketable strengths are, and how you can highlight them. Are you a performer? Are you technically amazing? Are you really, really attractive? Whatever the hook is, exploit it to the utmost, but don't go over the top. With your one-page bio, the best opening is a clear, distinct message or mission statement about what you do and where you want to take your art. Keep it short and succinct; business people usually don't have the time to read a long essay. Always consider the age, location, gender, and musical taste of your audience, and show your first draft to your friends for their input.

Remember to put your contact info on everything, and package your materials (if you're sending them by snail mail) in a simple, professional and eye-catching way. It's also a good idea to follow up with a phone call or email, just to confirm that your intended recipient received the package. When you're contacting journalists or magazine editors, remind them that you're available for interviews too. In every case, this is an opportunity for you to build relationships with the people you want to promote you and your brand.

Think Like an Entrepreneur

DJs aren't always savvy businessmen. We tend to think exclusively with a creative mind, rather than with the structured approach of a business manager. But if you carry yourself at all times as a professional, then promoters, bookers, and your audience will recognize your worth. Professionalism makes anyone attractive.

The top DJs build empires. Look at Above & Beyond, Armin van Buuren, Tiësto, and even DJ Vice. They produce music, write blog posts, host their own nights and remix competitions, share podcasts, sell merchandise, and in many cases even own their own record label. Hard work will pay off if you invest the time, but that's the key: you need to invest the time.

We can see some evidence of this by looking at Google Trends and studying how often the top DJs have been mentioned or referenced in online news. When we compare Google Trend results for Tiësto, deadmau5, Kaskade, Avicii, and Skrillex, a few patterns become readily apparent. Tiësto has remained steady for years, while deadmau5 started generating buzz in 2008 and seemed to peak in 2010. Avicii and Skrillex went through the roof in 2011 (and coincidentally, both were nominated for multiple Grammy awards the same year).

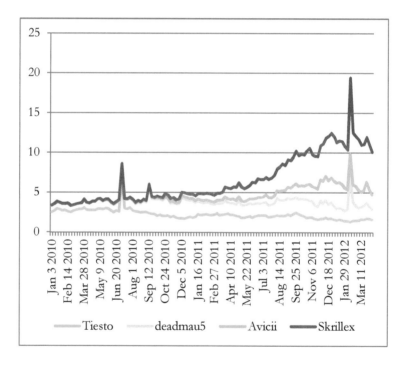

Tools like these can help you make sense of what's succeeding and what's failing. Online commerce can generate significant revenue for those who know how to take advantage of it, so if you want your share of the pie, you have to be ready to do the marketing research that will help your brand.

Differentiate Yourself

When you listen to a DJ mix, you've probably noticed that the more talented DJs can make good songs sound even better. It's in the way they mix the elements of the song, or in the way they use subtle effects to change the mood. The same song can sound very different, depending on the context of the mix.

Always push yourself to be creative with your equipment. Remember what we said in Chapter 6 about creating your sound; part of putting your personal stamp on a mix is to experiment with what you have. There's a reason why companies are crafting DJ gear with complex functionality. It's in your best interests to try out new features, effects and plug-ins whenever you can; you might discover the one quirk in the machine that will contribute to your signature sound.

A DJ should never be a human iPod. In a saturated DJ market, only a high-quality mix that displays overall technical ability, clever use of effects and an individual sound will get you noticed. But more importantly, playing the right tracks at the right points throughout the night will always outshine a technically flawless set. That ability can't be taught or even really *learned*; it takes instincts.

Always be yourself. Your favorite artists have achieved success because they're innovative and unique. It's okay to start out emulating your favorite artists, but if you limit yourself by mixing only with their style and sound in mind, you won't go very far. Instead of trying to replicate someone else's work, listen to their music and use it as inspiration.

Your role as a DJ is to build the atmosphere. Keep in mind that the term "peak hour" exists for a reason (usually between midnight and 2 a.m., when the venue is most crowded). Start off easy, read the crowd, and play what people want to hear. Eventually, you'll get to the hot new tracks you've been itching to play, but you need to make people *want* them to maximize the effect.

This is what it means to develop and curate your personal brand. It takes hard work. The music you play, the clothes you wear, your online presence, and your personality all factor into your image. Don't just copy your favorite DJ; instead, try to draw inspiration from a variety of sources, and add your own creative twist to differentiate yourself.

For up-and-coming DJs, we offer one parting piece of advice. Young DJs are often encouraged to learn multiple styles to get booked and play in various clubs, but this can be a negative, because people won't know what to expect when they come to your gigs. You aren't going to become globally famous by playing mashed-up top 40 hits. The best plan is to define and establish your brand, and then stick to it. Establish a niche, and *own* it. The genre of music you play doesn't have to define *how* you put it together.

13. Expand Your Reach with Social Media

At this point we all know how web-based and mobile technologies have transformed the way we communicate. With the advent of social media, a basic one-to-one dialogue somehow seems quaint and old-school. Interactive group conversations have become the way of the web.

But the stark naked truth is that if you have something to say, whether you're a DJ, a painter or a politician, it has to be worth hearing. Social media can be incredibly useful for expanding your brand online, but these tools are powerless without a message that's catered to the interests of the people you want to reach. To make your efforts *sticky*—to attract new people to you and your brand—you need to be conscious of what your existing (and potential) audience wants. That means interacting with them as often, and efficiently, as you can.

And by the way, don't forget that for all the virtual interaction that happens online, we live in a real world too. Talk to people at your gigs, and dance with the crowd when you're not playing. Go see other musicians and support the local scene. Be yourself and be authentic, and you'll find that people will want to listen to what you have to say.

Curating Your Online Presence

Setting up your blog, Facebook page or Twitter profile isn't the hard part. The real question is how do you generate activity? How do you establish a committed following, and then how do you engage with them?

Test the waters. Before you dive in, it's a good idea to familiarize yourself with what's happening in social media, especially with how it relates to music, technology and e-commerce. If you're new to Facebook and Twitter, follow the artist pages and feeds of the DJs you admire, and take note of what they're talking about. Visit their blogs if they have them, and seek out blogs by industry executives, music journalists and fans who are interested in your genre of music.

Sites like Mashable and Hypebot are also great places to find out what's trending in social media, technology and the music business in general. As always, information is power. There are trends in the music industry that you can capitalize on, and shifting consumer behavior patterns can present opportunities if you know where to find them (remember how Trent Reznor and Radiohead started a revolution by giving away music so they could attract fans who might buy the deluxe package?). It's always in your best interests to be open-minded and agile, so if a new approach, product or service hits the market and takes off, you're ready for it.

Engage your fans. When you start posting online, you need to be conscious of your tone of voice. You want to *engage* your fans, not lecture them. It's not just about communicating; it's about creating interactive exchanges and experiences that mean something. Imagine that you're following one of your favorite DJs. If he or she posts links to other blogs that you might find interesting, as well as music, photos, event invites, humorous links, and informed recommendations about films, art openings, books and other subjects, it's probably safe to say that you'll end up liking that DJ even more.

A good rule of thumb is to follow the late-night talk show rule. Think about the celebrity guests you see talking with Jay Leno or Jimmy Fallon. They tend to engage about broad human interest topics first (such as life stories or current affairs), and *then* they promote their book, movie, TV show, or event. This is a great model for building relationships through social media.[31]

If you want anyone to care about what you're selling, you have to engage them by being entertaining and informative. Your sphere of interest doesn't have to be exclusively focused on DJing and music; great stories and links to useful information and ideas that you find compelling are just as important. Once you get your fans hooked on the reality that you're a *regular person*, they'll be more receptive to your brand.

As a general rule of thumb, the content and updates that you post in online channels should follow a 4-to-1 ratio. Put simply, this means that for every social object (photos, Tweets, blog posts, audio/podcast clips, videos and status updates) that you post about yourself, you should post four more things that *aren't* about you.[32] And whatever they are, they need to be informative, inspirational, entertaining, engaging and/or remarkable.

---

[31] Steve Rubel. "The Clip Report" blog. Accessed March 12, 2012. [http://www.steverubel.me]

[32] Ramsey Mohsen. "How to Get Engagement on Facebook, Twitter or Your Blog," August 17, 2010. http://ramseymohsen.com/2010/08/how-to-get-engagement-on-facebook-twitter-or-your-blog.

It's not an exact science. The 4-to-1 rule is a simple set of guidelines to follow that will help you grow your fanbase and eventually "earn the right" to talk directly about what you're selling. This is how you build credibility, or *social currency*, with your fans and followers.

What We Learned from Using Email: It Still Works

Email is still a simple and cost-effective way to communicate with your fans. Email newsletters (or "blasts") are a great way to alert your fanbase about upcoming gigs and new music releases, and like your online posts, they can say a lot about you and your personality. Try not to be too serious or stilted in your tone—again, you want to draw people in, not push them away. Give them the facts, but feel free to embellish a bit with some humor whenever you can. Hone your message and get creative, and your fans will see you're having fun with it.

Never send unsolicited email. The last thing you want your name associated with is spam, because everyone hates it. Build an opt-in database by asking people for their email addresses, either in person at your gigs, or through a form on your website. Try to keep your email blasts to a respectable minimum; even if you have a lot of new gigs and releases coming up, it's best to send just two emails per month at the most, and usually early in the week (around Tuesday), which is when people tend to be most receptive.

To handle your bulk email blasts, we strongly recommend email client software from CampaignMonitor.com. It's inexpensive and provides a great service, including database management and analytics (Mixed In Key has used it since 2007).

To sum up, if you take the following steps, you're on your way to creating an effective email marketing campaign:

- **Create quality content**. A clear, concise message increases the chances that your recipient will read the email (and future emails). Make sure your subject heading is an attention-grabber (but *don't* use CAPS—it's annoying). Organize your content using lists and bullet points, especially for tour dates and appearances. Include a call for action to ensure your marketing piece will have an impact.[33]

- **Use an email sending service**. If you have more than 50 people on your mailing list, use a service like CampaignMonitor or MailChimp to automate and

---

[33] Matthew Toren. "How To Make Your Email Marketing Work – 5 Keys For Success," March 15, 2012.
http://www.youngentrepreneur.com/blog/how-to-make-your-email-marketing-work.

track the batch sending process. This is essential not just for tracking purposes, but also because it's possible your hand-emailed version will end up in your recipient's spam folder, and you run the risk of having your email account banned by your Internet service provider. Commercial services can send email in bulk without getting punished for it, because they obey strict anti-spam rules. Most services offer different pricing plans based on factors such as number of contacts and frequency of use.

- **Avoid looking like spam**. Place an "unsubscribe" button or link at the bottom of the email to give your recipients the choice to opt out. Make sure you are complying with laws such as the CAN-SPAM Act—no false headers or political/religious messages.

Getting Twitter to Work for You

Twitter is adding millions of new users every year, and their users conduct over 600 million searches on Twitter each day. More than one-third of Twitter users access the service through their mobile devices, making it an excellent way to tap into mobile markets.[34] You can use Twitter to

---

[34] Ibid.

post guest list promotions, news, and links to other sites, music streams, photos and video. It's an easy-to-use and free way to market yourself.

The question is, how do you get Twitter to *really* work for you? The key, as with any social media platform, is to curate your presence with a strategy in mind. If you have a website, you can start by posting your Twitter feed there, and including your website address in your Twitter bio (next to your profile pic). Cross-connections like these can help drive traffic to your website, but they're also important because they give potential fans multiple points of entry for learning more about you.

Building your followers on Twitter takes time and diligence. Stick to the 4:1 ratio we outlined above, and retweet posts that are interesting to you whenever you can; more often than not, you'll be rewarded with a new follower (or two). Take a look at the Twitter feeds of other DJs as well, and follow your favorites. If you're new to DJing, who knows? One of them might hear a mix set you posted, and invite you to open a gig.

Are You Using Facebook Wisely?

Facebook is a more popular small business tool than you might realize. Right now, over 100 million Facebook users are accessing Facebook through a mobile device.[35]

You can use a Facebook artist page to share new music or mixes you've recorded, as well as information about upcoming events. It's also a great place to post crowd shots of your gigs; if your fans see themselves in your photos, they might be inspired to post them on their own Facebook profiles and then tag them with the names of their friends.

Again, if you have a website, post a link to it under your **Contact Info**. You can also customize your navigation bar (in Facebook Timeline, it's the line of clickable options that runs across the top of the page) with links to your YouTube channel and your SoundCloud page, and you can give your fans the option to sign up for your email newsletter.

Facebook allows third-party developers such as RootMusic, ReverbNation and Bandcamp to provide musician profile apps, which have grown popular as more artists opt out of MySpace. Apps like these are worth researching if you want to customize your Page for playing

---

[35] Ibid.

music, posting tour information, and even selling merchandize. Facebook also maintains partnerships with Spotify, Rdio and other streaming services, making it clear that music-sharing has become central to the trajectory of social networking.

Managing Your YouTube Channel

YouTube adds an obvious visual aspect to marketing. Every day, more than two billion videos are viewed on YouTube; it's an especially effective way to reach the younger market.[36] You can use your YouTube channel to add a flashier and more entertaining aspect to your marketing efforts by posting videos from your shows, as well as how-to clips related to DJing. If you're into video editing programs like Final Cut Pro, you can also create a video montage for one of your mixes.

If you accumulate enough viewers, you can apply to become a YouTube Partner and start generating ad revenue from your videos. One way to build up your viewers is to use your other social media accounts—Facebook and Twitter especially—to announce when you've posted a new video. It's also a good idea to include a clickable link in any email blasts you send out.

---

[36] Ibid.

SoundCloud, FourSquare and Blogging

Sites like SoundCloud, Dubset, and Mixcloud are great resources for sharing music and mixes online. Location-based services like Foursquare can help you generate real-time buzz during an event. You might be able to work with a specific venue to offer deals or discounts to fans who check into your event through Foursquare.

Blogging is another smart way to engage with your audience. You can either embed a blog element in your website, or create an entirely separate site using templates from WordPress, Blogger or Tumblr.

It's okay to think of your blog as being a bit more open-ended than your website. You can post about events, giveaways and contests, but it's also a place where you can promote your interests and pursuits outside of music, and give your fans a glimpse of your true identity. If you enable commenting on your blog, be sure to tell your fans to keep their exchanges respectable—and keep an eye out for spammers (they love to flood comments sections with meaningless advertising).

Karl Detken: How to Navigate the Social Universe

As one of the key members of Pioneer's original development and marketing team behind the industry standard Pioneer CDJs, Karl Detken is a legend in the industry. During his nearly 20 years at Pioneer, he helped create more than 50 products, including the CDJ-2000 and the DJM-900 mixer. He's also a leading expert on social media, with over 300,000 followers on Twitter.

How did you get so deeply into social media?

KD: Basically, when I came out of Pioneer, I needed to keep myself busy. There was a lot of buzz about social media, so I decided to invest some time and study the dynamics of how social media works. I started with Twitter and I had about 14,000 followers from my years at Pioneer. I tweeted about the technology I knew about, and the life of professional DJs.

What I learned from social media is that it works as "inbound" marketing. People may not know the difference. Email blasts, websites and other "outbound" marketing methods are becoming less and less effective at being able to grow and keep a fanbase. Social media focuses on attracting and earning people's interest. You attract new fans that you may not have found otherwise by becoming a valuable source of information. Marketing used to be a one-way conversation, but social media is now a two-way conversation.

You have one of the biggest followings among DJs. Your recent Twitter follower count is over 300,000. That's a huge increase compared with your days at Pioneer. How did this happen?

KD: It took about 3 months for me to understand the dynamics here. I guess the catalyst for my growth was in figuring out how social media was meant to be used. I studied how some of my favorite Twitter members interacted with their audience. One thing that I learned is that I needed to find out what my audience is interested in. I consider social media platforms like Twitter, Facebook or YouTube as magazines. I would constantly look for relevant news and information. Content is king. The better your content is, the more it will be shared by your followers, and that's where the viral effect comes into play.

Your goal is to get retweeted by your followers. The more retweets, the bigger your message will get, and the more you will grow. That's the secret I learned really early on. And to give you an example of how crazy it can get, in December 2010, I received 42,000 retweets in one month. When you can do that, you're getting in front of more people. If you have something of value, they will follow you.

Does a higher follow count help the momentum?

KD: The first two thousand followers are relatively easy. Everything after that becomes a lot harder. When your audience sees that you grabbed 10,000 followers, it gives you more legitimacy. I found a couple of great Twitter power people, and basically what I do is study them and evaluate them. I would share their content and give them credit. Sometimes they would notice me, and I could ask them questions. Eventually, they started retweeting me. For a DJ, initially, it's a good idea to find a couple of people to study and see how they are growing their audience, and how they choose what content to post. Find an expert who you respect.

As I said before, content is king. A great way to connect with your audience is to give away music. If you think about it, music is a really intimate thing. The artist puts their soul into every composition, and it makes them vulnerable. If you give away these kinds of gifts, you actually start building an audience. It's the same with giving away passes to a show. It's important to create that engagement and be accessible to your audience. It's nice to see someone who's down to earth, who's cool, and who has something of value to give to his audience.

The idea is to create something special for the artist. Kaskade Music Monday is an example where he posts a new track every week. It's the same idea that Morgan Page is doing with his Twitter account. I asked Morgan, "What are you an expert at?" He came to the conclusion that he might have some ideas about production that were worth sharing. I told him, "Do it! Your audience will love it and will find it useful." So he came up with #MPTips (Morgan Page Tips). He would share production tips, gear ideas, touring and performance ideas—I thought it was brilliant. I remember he talked about drinking a bottle of water during the end of his set, so you wouldn't be dehydrated, and your performance could be better. He got exactly what social media is about.

Do these ideas still apply to Twitter, Facebook and all other social networks?

KD: Absolutely. The reason you want to be on all the platforms is because your entire audience may not be on Twitter or YouTube, and you want to have as much coverage as possible. You don't have to spend a lot of time in each one. You can set up your accounts to cross-post from one account to the others. The key is to be relevant to your audience and to be a source of useful information.

So let's say you're a DJ who's new to the business, and you don't know where to start. What I always encourage DJs to do other than becoming relevant and sharing things, is trying to understand who your audience is. When I started off, I was just talking to DJs and giving them Pioneer ideas and Pioneer stories. What I started to realize is that it's a narrow niche. In order to grow beyond that, you need to find people who have regular lives. When I expanded what I was talking about, I started growing a lot faster. I became interesting to more people. I figured out how often I should post new information. This is something you have to test out. If you post too much, you'll annoy your audience and they may leave. The sweet spot for me is to tweet every four hours. Some tweets are technology-based, and some are lifestyle-based.

You post a lot of inspirational quotes and positive content, and you come across as a nice guy. It doesn't seem like you'd ever say something like, "Oh man, I'm waiting in line at the DMV again." Should the message be positive most of the time?

KD: Absolutely it should be positive, because A) you might offend someone if it's not, and B) you should look at yourself as a magazine. You just won't see complaints like that in a real magazine; one magazine wouldn't complain about another. A lot of touring DJs make the mistake of talking about themselves too much. Nobody really cares that you're having a ham sandwich; you want to talk about other things. It's also never a good idea to say negative things about other DJs or other styles of music, because you run the risk of alienating your fans.

What gave famous DJs such a huge boost on social media? They have massive followings now—what led to that?

KD: Any of the big DJs will naturally have a large following. I think these are guys who really "get" social media. Some set themselves apart because they share their heart and soul with their fans; they aren't just sharing their itinerary and schedule. Fans want to know that their idol is a regular guy.

I've noticed that BT posts a lot of photos on social media. It has been statistically proven that posting photos on Facebook has a more profound effect than any piece of text you could normally post. Multimedia will be more viral than any kind of text you can put out. Kaskade brought a guy with him on tour to film the shows, and those videos went viral because people wanted to get the behind-the-scenes vibe. It's good to share the normalcy of being this superstar DJ.

For young DJs who have a small following now and want to get deeper into social media, what's the BEST piece of advice you can give them?

KD: The core thing for me is something that I call the Power of the Five E's:

- **Engage**: Connect with your audience.

- **Educate**: Give them something of value that you're an expert in.

- **Entertain**: Give them something outside of your normal posts, like jokes or inspiration.

- **Evaluate**: Are you growing or not growing? Are you tweeting enough or too much?

- **Empower**: Enable your fans to become evangelists. You want them to be talking about you more than you talk about yourself. When you harvest the power of word-of-mouth, at that point, you'll see exactly what social media is about.

14. Work with Your DJ Team

With every aspect of DJ culture generating more revenue than ever, it's a good time to be behind the decks if you're at the top of the food chain. A globe-trotting superstar like Tiësto can pull down as much as $20 million a year[37]—a far cry from the post-recessionary rave years of the '90s, when being underground was a badge of honor, but also meant that you had to scramble to make what you could just to cover the rent.

The reality is that the DJ pay scale varies widely.[38] At one end of the spectrum, many DJs are willing to work for free just to get their foot in the door. On the other, superstar DJs earn more than $50,000 per night. But if you consider yourself a working DJ, and you're spinning for five hours and making $300, does that really translate to $60 an hour? You may only be in the booth from 10 p.m. to 3 a.m., but the pre-party preparation that goes into DJing can be a full-time job by itself.

---

[37] Jim Fusilli. "Tiësto: Electronic Music's Superstar," *The Wall Street Journal*, March 30, 2011.

[38] "Time Is Money: DJ Salaries," August 2001. http://www.discjockey101.com/aug2001.html.

When you make the decision to commit to your dream of being a professional DJ, these are the key questions you need to ask yourself:

- How many hours per week do I spend reading music blogs and magazines, researching music, preparing tracks, setting cue points, practicing transitions, and preparing for gigs?

- How much money have I invested in new equipment, including headphones, computers, music, backpacks, hardware, or even clothes?

- How much time do I spend promoting my nights to friends and fans?

- How much revenue is the club generating because customers like my music?

- How much of that $300 will pay for my health insurance and taxes?

The expenses don't even end there. Many DJs will spend hours networking and meeting with club managers or promoters every week. Others will travel long distances to gigs and pay the cost out of their own pocket.

Before you eagerly accept a low-paying gig just to get in a club's good graces, consider the precedent you're setting about cost and value of your time. If you work for cheap, you're branding yourself to be booked for cheap in the future. Don't sell yourself short; you're an artist and you deserve to be paid for your talent. Research trends in your market and determine a fair market price, and don't be afraid to ask for the money you deserve. With hard work, eventually you'll get to the point where you'll need to consider building a team of professionals around you.

Pros and Cons of DJing Full-time

The pros of being a full-time DJ are pretty clear. You're getting paid to do something you love, and to play music and interact with fans on a regular basis. By DJing regularly, you can build up your chops and accumulate experience, with more opportunities to test new songs and new mixing techniques. You'll also get to meet more people in the industry, which will help you establish a name for yourself and prove that you're committed to your craft.

And then there are the cons. To pay the bills, you might have to accept gigs working at venues you don't like, playing music you don't want to play. You aren't covered by medical insurance, so you'll have to pay out-of-pocket expenses. Taxation is also tricky. Yes, you can write off a lot of your expenses as a small business owner, but you have to track receipts closely throughout the year. Since most of your gigs will not take taxes out of your income, you will likely have to pay a large lump sum in taxes at the end of the year. The best advice we can offer: be prepared to manage your finances wisely.

Interview with Ash Pournouri:
Avicii's Manager

As the CEO of At Night Management, Ash Pournouri has shown he has the magic touch when it comes to helping his artists develop their careers. His highest-profile client is Grammy-nominated DJ Avicii (whose aliases also include Tim Berg and Tom Hangs). As one of the youngest DJs on the international dance music scene, Avicii is on track to become a legend.

In this book, we cover the roles of different people in the music industry. Please tell us about your job. What kind of support do you offer Avicii?

AP: I would say that Tim and I have a professional relationship that far exceeds the manager role. My services go beyond normal management in the sense that I get involved in every aspect of my artist's life. Tim himself has referred to me as his second father, extra brother, friend, and mentor. I want what's best for Tim's talent, and that is to sometimes get involved when he's stuck creatively to help him develop his sound. I take everything that doesn't have to do with music production off his hands. It's a lot of work for a manager, but we've proven that it works and that it can super-boost an artist's career.

How did the two of you meet, and how did this partnership begin?

AP: I found him on some blogs online. I was never looking for a client. I had no intention of being a manager. When I got in touch with him I was more or less curious about what I could offer creatively to help someone who I thought was talented but needed direction. We met, hit it off, tried some production work together—and the rest is history.

You're part of a unique team: most managers are not closely involved in their artist's careers. In your case, it looks like a 50/50 partnership. What do you see as a useful benefit of that?

AP: It is more than a 50/50 partnership because I'll do whatever I have to do to make sure my artist's career progresses and rises to be the best it can be. However, the financial terms are that of any standard management deal, so I guess we were very lucky to find each other.

What do you think caused clubs' demand for him to skyrocket?

AP: First of all, I believe an artist has three legs of strategy that can be built up separately but make use of each other. One is music, one is performance, and one is brand/profile. They can all be monetized with the right strategy, and you can have unbalanced success in them too. I think everything we've accomplished is a milestone of its own in all those three legs, and we've pushed hard to make sure no leg is lagging.

At what point do you think a DJ can afford to hire a manager?

AP: As soon as you decide you're serious about a career in entertainment, you should look for a manager. A good manager will help create opportunities and sell your talent to the rest of the world. It's never too early or too late for that! A manager takes a cut from your income, so essentially a good manager should MAKE you money, not the other way around. If that money is not being made, drop your manager fast.

Do You Need an Agent?

As Ash Pournouri points out, a manager takes a cut of your income—traditionally around 15 percent—so you need to take that into account if you're just starting out. In the beginning, a manager will help you negotiate the best terms for your gigs, but once you reach a certain level of brand saturation in your market, the idea of hiring a booking agent to help you branch out into other markets might look like a reasonable prospect.

But before you even think about taking this step, it's important to consider two basic questions: How does an agency make money, and how are you going to benefit the agency? For example, if an agent wants to make $50,000 per year, and takes a 10 percent cut from each DJ gig he books, he would need to book a DJ at least 500 times at $1000 per night just to make his gross annual salary (that's before taxes). So put yourself in the agent's shoes. Can you generate enough work to justify that business relationship?

Put simply, an agency is probably not the way to go unless you have the potential to secure global bookings.

You don't need an agent's help if you're just playing in one city. Agents only come into play when you're negotiating with big clubs, in multiple cities.

So how do you make it without having a huge agency like AM Only behind you? One way to improve your chances of getting booked is to network with the general managers at clubs. You want to let them know you're a professional, and you're available. If you make a good impression, and if they ever need you at the last minute (which happens more often than you might think on the club circuit), you'll get the call, and then you're on your way.

15. Where to Go From Here

We hope that all the topics we've covered in this book, from mixing techniques to marketing approaches and business practices, have given you a clearer idea of what it takes to be a better DJ. To elaborate on a point that world-class manager Ash Pournouri makes in our interview with him (Chapter 14), there are three paths to success for every professional DJ: get musical with your mixing, hone your performance skills (and crowd instincts), and curate your brand.

When you think about yourself as a DJ, it's crucial to identify what you're great at, and then move forward. (As we've said before: pick a niche, and then *own* it.). Once you're comfortable with the music you play and what you can do with it, the other paths to success—performance and brand—will follow.

So to sum up, if you want to improve the musical aspect of your repertoire, here's what we recommend:

- Learn all the tricks of advanced DJing—harmonic mixing, energy level mixing, energy boosts and mashups.

- Follow the latest trends in music, but make sure you have an ample collection of classics.

- Be adventurous with your music choices. It's important to know the latest bangers and club staples, but you need to stand out from other DJs too. Stock your music library with unique and eclectic material.

- Understand the progression of music throughout the night, and be ready to play in any time slot.

To improve your performance chops, remember these steps:

- Get a feel for what creates a great experience for your fans.

- Make sure you have a reliable DJ equipment setup that you can count on.

- Always have a "rescue plan" so you can keep playing if something goes wrong.

- Make backups of your music and be able to use them in any situation.

- Familiarize yourself with the roles of everyone in the club scene, respect their hard work, and do what you can to keep them happy.

Finally, to improve your brand, focus on the four main aspects of marketing:

- Design a simple but eye-catching DJ logo for yourself.

- Get your promotional pictures done so they look as professional as you can make them, regardless of your budget.

- Carry business cards that are high-quality, simple and sleek.

- Launch a Facebook page where you engage your fans with frequent updates and useful posts—not just about you and your music, but about anything that might interest the people who follow you.

It's entirely possible to make a career out of being a DJ. As we can assure you, it's an amazing feeling to play in front of a live audience. All the information in this book is intended to support your efforts and improve your chances for success.

On that note, if anything you've learned here has contributed to your success story, we want to hear about it. Please post it anywhere online and let us know…and keep mixing!

Please Review This Book!

If you found this book useful, please post a review on Amazon. Reviews are hard for authors to get, and we would sincerely appreciate your help.

Credits

First and foremost, a sincere "thank you" to thousands of Mixed In Key fans who told their friends about our software. We have a fantastic community of DJs who use Mixed In Key, and we appreciate all the feedback and ideas that we receive every day.

We want to thank a remarkable group of people whose work had a big impact on this book. Thank you to:

Above & Beyond * Allen & Heath * Andrew Aziz * Andrew Madsen * Andy Rigby-Jones * Antonio Diaz * Ash Pournouri * A-Trak * Axwell * Beatport * Betsy Magde * Bill Murphy * Biz Martinez * Brian Tappert * Brooks Pettus * BT * Cathy Guetta * Chad Pranke * David Guetta * Debbie Maxted * Devin Ludlow * DJ Download * DJ Prince * Dubfire * Ed Carruthers * Endo (Mike Henderson) * Enferno * Eric Jensen * Glen Scott at 1010 Collective * Heather Schulz * Hernan Cattaneo * High Contrast * Jeremy Sallee * Joe Ok * Joe Sill * John Digweed * John Steventon * Jonas Tempel * Joona Puurunen * Karl Detken * Kaskade * Kendall Woodford * Kristin Walinski * Laurialie Pow * Louis Ng * Mark Davis * Mark Walker * Markus Schulz * Martin Douglas * Meta Weiss * Mike Levine * Morgan Page * Native Instruments * Nick Warren * Olga Kaganova * Patrick Machielse *

Paul Oakenfold * Paul van Dyk * Pete Tong * Phil at Digital DJ Tips * Samuel Jack * Sara Griggs * Sasha * Sebastien Gabriel * Sebastian Ingrosso * Serato * Stephanie LaFera * Steve Angello * Traxsource * Victor Vorobyev * zplane development